Praise for Chris Heivly

JUD BOWMAN
Founder and CEO of Appia ($100M exit) and
Co-Founder and CTO of Motricity ($1.2B IPO)
"Chris brings real world entrepreneurial experience to
the table as a co-founder of MapQuest (and The Startup
Factory), and talks frankly about success and failure in a
way that uniquely resonates with startup entrepreneurs."

PORTER BAYNE
Founder and CEO of Antenna
"Chris has a uniquely good understanding of the human
side of starting something. He's not afraid to discuss fear.
He helps minimize drama and bullshit. He pushes you to
plan just enough and execute a lot, to see how your market
really responds. He views early success and struggles
simply as something to consider. And he makes you laugh,
which helps you keep on an even keel."

RYAN ALLIS
CEO and Co-Founder of iContact ($170M exit);
Chairman & Co-Founder of Connect and Hive
"Chris's thought leadership extends far beyond the pages
of this book. But if you are not lucky enough to hear
him speak or go through his Startup Factory mentorship
program, then this book is your best way to get a bit of his
insight, humor and inspiration to take the leap yourself."

JAMES AVERY
Founder and CEO of Adzerk,
Managing Director of Zerk Media
"Chris took Adzerk under his wing at an early stage so I got to see first hand how Chris's passion and knowledge can help a startup and CEO grow. Some do it for the money, some do it for the fame, Chris does it because of his burning passion to help startups succeed."

VIKRAM RAO
Co-Founder and Co-CEO of Tuee (TSF investment)
"Chris was instrumental in helping us launch, grow, and ultimately sell our company. He draws upon his years of startup experience to help his portfolio companies solve any challenge they come across. He can simplify even the most complex of challenges to actionable takeaways—and he does it all with a goofy smile and the utmost humility."

SARA CAPRA
Co-Founder and Chief Commercial Officer of Orate (TSF investment)
"Chris Heivly is open-minded, helpful, and candid. He has a unique background, being an intrapreneur, entrepreneur, and now mentor to other entrepreneurs. This allows for a unique and valuable perspective in a variety of areas that new entrepreneurs can use to progress in their own business. I always appreciate that Chris uses personal anecdotes of successes and failures to educate entrepreneurs, and help them achieve the same level of success or avoid the same fate."

ROBBIE ALLEN
Founder and CEO of Automated Insights
"Chris is one of the rare few in the startup world that has built an amazing organization that helps startups and connects thousands of people around a common cause of entrepreneurship."

JON FRANGAKIS
Co-Founder and CEO if Mira (TSF investment)
"Chris doesn't subscribe to the fads and buzzwords
that are so prevalent throughout startup-land today. He
knows that, above all else, the only thing that matters
is traction. He was the one that pushed us to achieve
"one full crank" of the company's business model to
prove out its technology during our MVP and it made
all the difference in us getting funded and on our way to
product-market fit. When we look back on our journey
through the earliest days of our company, I know that
any success we find will be directly attributable in part
to Chris' mentorship and guidance."

F. SCOTT MOODY
*Co-Founder, Chairman, CEO of AuthenTec (sold to
Apple), Co-Founder and CEO of K4Connect*
"Chris is a "been there, done that" kind of guy when
it comes to startups. From his own highly successful
startup, to leading a venture capital firm, to running a
successful accelerator, to personally mentoring hundreds
of entrepreneurs, Chris is not only someone that knows his
stuff, but is the kind of person that truly cares."

PATRICK MATOS
Co-Founder and CEO of CareLuLu (TSF Investment)
"Chris pushes entrepreneurs to constantly challenge their
assumptions about their business and their customers.
Many startup 'advisors' tout the lean startup approach and
tell founders that customer development is important, but
Chris and The Startup Factory actually force you to do it.
EVERY DAY. Chris has been in the entrepreneur's shoes,
and can give real-life actionable advice. Plus, he's funny
(sometimes ;)"

Build The Fort

Why 5 simple lessons

you learned as a 10-year-old

can set you up for startup success.

Chris Heivly

Lisa Hagan Books

Publisher: Lisa Hagan Books

For information about special discounts for bulk purchases, please reach us through, www.lisahaganbooks.com

Designed by Smythtype Design

ISBN 978-0-9764986-3-6

Dedication

To my Dad,
who read four to five books per week
during his adult life and still influences me every day,
and Patty, who has offered unwavering support
through every one of my crazy passions.

This is for both of you.

Table of Contents

Introduction

I have built industry-leading products, founded and co-founded startup businesses, been recruited to captain existing businesses ranging in size from $200K to $20M in revenue, and invested and managed more than $75M in early-stage companies for a multibillion dollar corporation. I now operate the premier seed investment fund in the Southeast focused on startups and first-time founders.

I am an entrepreneur, an intrapreneur, an investor, and a community leader.

I was you once.

Starting your own company has never been sexier than it is today. Every week, you read countless stories about the newest Mark Zuckerberg that celebrate freshly minted millionaires in this supercharged startup dream for budding entrepreneurs. The great news is that you can live this dream today. The dream knows no boundaries, regardless of age, gender, geographic location, or education achievement. Entrepreneurs are sprouting everywhere.

This is the foundation of the New Economy and if you are so inclined — it's time to get in the game.

Yet today I would imagine that more than half of you would-be startup founders stay inside the dream and never make the leap into reality. And those who do and "risk it all" typically do so with unrealistic notions of how to maximize those first delicate steps into entrepreneurship.

Many books, blogs, community programs, and new-age investment vehicles are available to you as a budding entrepreneur. The intent with most of these is to develop your business-building muscles. However, most focus on later-stage business building and not the initial decision to leap and those first critical steps. Most are vehicles organized from a point of view that assumes you already understand the language and pain points of business building.

But by definition, as a first-time entrepreneur you have no context, feeling, or understanding of the initial stages of business building.

Build the Fort takes a step back from these books and takes a simpler tack.

I believe that the lessons you learned and applied as a 10-year-old with the simple task of "building a fort" can be applied to launching the company you always wanted.

By orienting your mental framework as a 10-year-old and focusing on the leap and those first critical steps, I posit that you will place yourself in a better position. Over the course of this book, I will break down my personal fort-building experiences and use them as an analogy for my journey of building MapQuest as well as The Startup Factory.

MapQuest was a long ride that began years before the Internet. We started with software preloaded on PCs, then on CD-ROM, and eventually the website you all immediately gravitated to. Since then, I have worked with hundreds of entrepreneurs just like you. Today, my partner Dave Neal and I operate The Startup Factory, which invests $50K to $100K in startup companies and matches those investment dollars with an equal amount of mentorship.

We can't take every one of you on at TSF as an investment. However, I can share with you observations and personal lessons gleaned over my 30+ years. I hope that this book can inspire you as well as provide direction on your startup journey.

Build the Fort outlines five basic elements that are common to fort building and starting up your first company. These five elements are simple to understand and provide the reader a foundation for a successful launch. I will also outline critical personal decisions and tools that you can use to become the best fort builder.

Whether you are 16 or 60, male or female, from Poughkeepsie or Paris, *Build the Fort* will provide you a better understanding of the earliest microsteps for starting your own business by overlaying my 30 years of experiences in startups, investments, big-company intrapreneurship, community development, and of course, fort building with my childhood friends.

My Favorite Fort

In Newtown Square, PA, at the end of Doe Lane, a 20-acre tract of land had all the elements any kid would kill for: thickly wooded trees on an unbuildable steep hill with a meandering creek. Forty years later it has still not been built upon due to the hilly topography. The "woods," as we called it, was far enough away from our homes to be ours and not our parents' (no parent would ever wander over there), and close enough that we did not have to trek far to it or freak our parents out by being too far away from home. We were basically within shouting distance.

"Chris, Tim, Marc — time for dinner," my mother would call out.

It was our world and we spent hours there. I mean major hours. Like leave your house at 8:00 in the morning and return for dinner and yet your Mom knew you had been fed somewhere and that you were safe. The woods were our suburban playground. It is where I first started building forts.

There were about 25 kids in our neighborhood at the end of two cul-de-sacs that cut us off from any regular street traffic. Nobody could cut through to get to anywhere else. This road layout really insulated us and created our private world of adventure. We were limited only by our imagination. Really. I know it sounds corny. Stay with me.

The kids in the neighborhood I counted as friends ranged in age from two years older to four years younger than me. So about a six-year range. Kenny Doyle and Robert Wynn were on the older side and really did not engage with us much at all. My youngest brother Marc's age group, which included Chucky Doyle, Jeff Linton, and a few others, sometimes hung around, especially when we were involved in a game of kick-the-can after dinner. In between, we had my middle brother Timmy as well as Danny Moore, John Durand, David Stackhouse, and Jimmy Mickey. I hope you have figured out by now that adding a "y" to the end of your name was an integral part of our neighborhood experience. (It wasn't just limited to the boys — right, Patsy?)

Jimmy Doyle's house was the closest to the woods so, in some ways, the Doyles were the gatekeepers since everything passed by them on the way to the one real entrance at the end of Doe Lane.

At 10 years old, give or take a couple years, Jimmy Doyle and I would sit and scheme about building a fort. Forts are cool for boys and girls alike and Jimmy and I built a lot of forts. We built forts into the hill, we built forts on flat land, and we tried to build a fort in a couple of trees but that turned out to be pretty hard.

All told, I would not be surprised if we built 20 forts over a four- to five-year period.

I believe it is human nature to want a private place that you can call your own. There is a real sense of independence that comes with four walls and a ceiling. For a 10-year-old, it is the fort. When you are in your fort you feel like you are the King or Queen of Your Domain. Nothing is cooler than a couple 10-year-olds sitting around looking for a spot in the woods dreaming of what could be. This fort is your place.

"Hey Chrissy," Jimmy called out. "Wanna build a fort?"

"Sounds fun, what do you have in mind this time?" I replied.

Jimmy stood up and explained, "Well, our old fort is pretty run down, we barely have a roof so when it rains we can't use the fort, and it's kind of small; it can only hold the two of us at any one time. The thing I hate most about all of our forts is that they look like a bunch of 8-year-olds built them. I want something better!"

His words really resonated with me for some reason. It was one of those moments where you go to a new level or place in your head. I guess it was like growing up.

I jumped in, "Yeah, I hate the leaking roof as well. Whenever it rains, we can't use the fort for like three days. And we certainly can't store anything in our fort or it will be ruined. Where are you thinking we should build this time—the same place or somewhere new? Should we use the same stuff from the old fort?"

"I was checking out that house they are building up the street and it looks like they have a pile of scrap wood ready to get rid of and I think a bunch of those pieces would make for a new fort," Jimmy added excitedly. He was starting to get into it as his voice increased in both volume and urgency.

I countered with equal passion, "You know what, Jimmy. My Dad has this tarp he was using up at the Little League field that he's not using anymore. I bet that would make a great cover for the ceiling so when it rains we won't get wet anymore."

"Fantastic," Jimmy said. "Let's go scout some areas!"

"Sounds great. But before we go I had another thought. You know how we always build down in that hollow near your house that is always damp and muggy and filled with bugs? What do you think about looking for a spot up on the hill?"

With that, off we would go to walk the woods for the one-hundredth time. Each foray into the woods seemed to give us a fresh perspective on our fort-building goal.

"What if we dug into the hill up in that open area about halfway up the mountain (maybe it was a 75' elevation difference, but we were 10 so it looked like Everest).

"We would get a great view of the neighborhood and there already is a little cut-out right off that main path we always use," I added.

"I bet if we asked your brother Timmy he would help us haul the wood up. He's the strongest and Danny's

Dad just got done building that deck around his pool. Why don't we ask him to be in the fort with us and he can get a hammer and some nails?" Jimmy said.

Jimmy and I approached Danny that afternoon after we had scouted the new destination.

"Hey Danny, wanna build a fort with us? We found a great spot up in the woods right off that main path that looks right down on your house and Jimmy found some wood we can use. I got Timmy to help us carry the wood. We are hoping that you can get some leftover nails from your Dad as well as help us dig out the hole on the side of the hill. Whaddya think?" I asked him with every serious bone in my body.

We were talking about a two- to three-day effort and total commitment to the fort was critical. There was no room for fence sitters in my mind. Danny was never one for a total commitment as he liked to be more of a lone wolf, and I think he got bored quicker than everyone else.

So off we went with Jimmy, Danny, Timmy, and me to build a fort in the woods off Doe Lane in Newton Square, PA, in the summer of 1970.

First things first. I told the guys, we have to get all of the wood from the lot up the street before they take it to the dump or someone else decides to borrow it.

"Let's wait a couple hours until the builders go home just in case they don't want us to take the wood. Until then let's start clearing the area that Jimmy and I found."

Off we trudged to the woods with a few shovels borrowed from our respective sheds or garages. The work was hard as we were just 10 years old and there is only so much leverage you can create with 50 pounds of weight.

The idea was to carve out an area about 6 feet wide and dig into the hill about 3 feet.

"Hey Danny, why don't you work the far side of the hole with Timmy and Chrissy and I will work this side of the hole. That way we can take turns using the two shovels," Jimmy shared with the guys.

Danny countered, "Where do you want to put the dirt? I think if we throw it to the side, we can use it later to help strengthen the walls there."

"That's a great idea!" we all exclaimed.

That day we were able to dig out enough of a hole in the side of the hill to give us a solid dirt wall for the back of the fort and some pretty good sidewalls. Certainly the digging had provided enough of a foundation that we could add walls from the wood we were going to "borrow" from the new house site up the street.

As we watched the builders head home late in the afternoon but before our dinnertime, we all ran down the path and up the street to the lot where we proceeded to inventory the scrap wood.

It took us about 45 minutes and something like three or four trips back and forth to get all the scrap wood up there. As we were getting the last few pieces Jimmy stopped us for a second.

"I am not sure how many pieces we need or whether we need every piece here. But what I am thinking is that we make one more trip to bring more than we need just in case. I know we are all tired but this will give us all the wood we should ever need."

We could always count on Jimmy to push us that extra little bit.

The next day we all met at Jimmy's house at about 8 a.m. Nothing was said the night before, we all just woke up excited to get started on the next phase of fort building. It turns out that Jimmy had already made it up to the new fort and had organized the wood into piles. Armed with energy and passion, we proceeded to dig holes for wall supports and then attached the pieces of plywood to the 2 x 4 inch studs that were going in the holes.

"Hey guys," Danny said, "the studs keep moving and I can't get the nails to go in right. I am not sure what to do."

We all stopped for a few minutes trying to figure out what to do next.

My brother jumped in, "I got an idea. Why don't we pull the studs out of the holes and lay them on the ground and then nail in the plywood first and then put the whole wall (studs and plywood) back in the ground with the entire wall intact. I saw them do that when they built that addition to your house a few years ago, Danny."

And with that, we had ourselves a couple of wood sidewalls to go along with our dirt back wall. We ended up having to re-dig the loose dirt we had added when we put the studs in first. This ended up setting us back an hour or so but the walls were much sturdier and that was what really mattered.

With three walls completed (the back dirt wall and the two plywood sidewalls), attention now centered on the roof. In all of my fort building, it was always the roof that was the weak point of the structure. The problem came from either a lack of sturdy materials and/or an inability to create a sturdy structure from the available materials. Again, be gentle on us; we were 10.

In addition to our roof design inexperience, we realized that we did not have enough plywood to cover the entire roof. We were dealing with scraps of plywood. If there were two full pieces of 4 x 8 feet (the way it comes from Home Depot now), we could have made that work. But we were going to have to cobble together a bunch of random pieces of plywood to make one roof that was about 8 x 8 feet. And we had no saw from which to cut pieces to size. We needed some really good ideas now.

"How about stringing the tarp across and making that the roof," Jimmy wondered.

"Sounds good but how do we keep it from blowing away?" I asked. "And the last time we tried something like that, the tarp sagged in the middle. We could try and put something in the middle of the fort like a teepee."

Timmy spoke up for the first time, "I hate the tarp plan as the only part of the roof. Every time we build a fort we half-ass the roof. I would like to find a way to make a roof that really works and that looks like a roof like our houses. Then we can add the tarp by laying it over the wood to keep out the rain. I think we should find more plywood and 2 x 4s and make a real roof!"

He was on a roll.

Timmy hardly ever spoke up so his insistence to push ourselves to make something better was heard and felt by all of us. If he felt strong enough to voice this, we should listen and consider his idea.

"Where can we find some more wood?" I asked everyone. "I think we need to think beyond the scrap pile where we got all of this."

There were basically four paths out of our little world. We could head out either end of the woods—basically following either the entrance or exit of the creek—into two completely different but much larger neighborhoods. We did not know these areas that well at all.

The third choice was to head out between the two houses at the end of the cul-de-sac into a neighborhood similar to ours that eventually came to the retail area of Newtown Square on West Chester Pike. We were more familiar with this area as we cut through here to get to the corner store where we bought candy, Tastycakes, soda, and chips. The last exit was out of the entrance to our double cul-de-sac into a couple neighborhoods that we knew the best because we drove through here whenever we were with our families.

I have always been the organizer it seems, so I laid out a rough plan.

"Why don't we split into two groups and explore the two neighborhoods that we are most familiar with," I asked somewhat rhetorically. "Jimmy and I will head up this way, and Danny and Timmy you head out the far end of the woods towards West Chester Pike. We are looking for 2 x 4s and plywood. We'll meet back here sometime this afternoon."

"Don't tell your Moms because we might get in trouble for leaving the woods," Danny added.

He was always a little nervous, especially when operating outside our comfort area. Later in life he was probably the last one of us to try beer. Later we knew to refer to it as Catholic guilt. I saw it play out as a kid and I saw it play out as a teenager down at the Jersey shore. It was just Danny.

So, off we all went in teams of two heading in completely opposite directions on a mission to find, borrow, and possibly steal some wood for our fort. I was always amazed at what we could find if we looked hard enough. There was always some building project that had some extra wood lying around. (At least it looked mostly extra to us.) Behind sheds, we would find some interesting material that the homeowner thought he would use someday, but we all knew that was not going to happen.

We were now in serious asset-gathering mode and this called for the full-team effort. Depending on the amount of stuff and the size, we either grabbed it while we were exploring, or doubled-back with the other guys. We hauled some stuff back up the hill to the fort right before dinner.

Jimmy and I were able to find some extra wood in a couple of different places, including what turned out to be a key donation from a neighbor. You see while scavenging through back yards, Jimmy and I ran across some old plywood behind the shed of Mr. Conti. As we stared at the wood, we knew we had a big dilemma: take the wood or ask permission. I have to be honest with you that we typically would not ask permission and may not have this time either but Mr. Conti saw us from his kitchen window. He waved with a great big smile.

"Hi Mr. Conti!" we shouted. "We are searching for scrap wood so we can build a fort. It should be the best fort we have built so far and we are short some wood."

Mr. Conti was retired, I guess, and had the nicest lawn and back yard of anyone in the neighborhood. He had a pool, and a horseshoe pit with real sand held in place by a wood frame. For a while a few years back, we were all afraid of him as he and his wife had no kids, which was weird. We had since broken through that fear when they invited us to swim in his pool. If that is not an icebreaker for a couple of sweaty kids, I don't know what is.

Out Mr. Conti came from his house.

"So you are building a fort, huh? What makes this one the best, boys?"

I jumped in, "Normally we just throw some things together, but this time we have some real wood from that house they are building around the corner and Danny's Dad gave us some extra nails. We have built the walls but are having trouble figuring out how to build a good roof. We have a tarp but we want to use that to cover the roof to keep out the rain, not to make the roof."

By this time, Timmy and Danny had joined us.

"Well boys, maybe I can help you figure out how to build a roof. Would you like some help? I may know a little bit about building things as I built that shed you see there against the house as well as that little pool house that covers the pool equipment."

I looked at the guys, they looked at me, and I think we all had the same thought — Mr. Conti could help us build a real roof for our fort.

We all answered at the same time, "Yes! We would love some help!"

"OK boys, tell me what you got so far and we can figure this out together," Mr. Conti said. He was pretty serious like this was his job or something. We all got pretty serious too.

I started: "You see we have dug a hole into the hill about halfway up the hill in the woods over there. So we have a back wall of dirt to start. Then we took some plywood and a couple of 2 x 4s and built two walls. We dug some holes and leveled out the side and put the walls in the ground and filled the dirt back into the holes. And we have some leftover wood up at the fort."

Jimmy was getting excited now and jumped in as soon as I was done: "We nailed the plywood to the 2 x 4s so that there is about a foot of 2 x 4 sticking out the bottom of each wall so we could just slide the whole wall into the holes."

He was very proud of what we had accomplished so far.

Timmy grabbed a couple sticks to start drawing in the dirt.

"We want to build a real roof to sit on top of the walls that is really sturdy, right? I was figuring that we could rest the roof on the dirt in the back of the fort and then on a 2 x 4 running along the front of the fort that connects the two walls," Timmy added. "What do you think?"

"The first thing we need to do, boys, is figure out what we have to work with," Mr. Conti said. "I have a few ideas but it depends on what kind of wood you have and how much you got. If you guys don't mind, can you bring all the wood you have so far over to my back yard and then we can figure out a plan together to build this roof?"

That afternoon, the four of us took about three trips to the fort, climbed up the hill, grabbed the lumber, and then walked down the hill and over a couple houses to Mr. Conti's lawn. It was tiring but we did it. Mrs. Conti came out when we were done with lemonade for each one of us.

"Great job boys," Mr. Conti said. "We have a lot to work with here and I am confident that we can make this new fort. We can get started tomorrow morning. Get a good night's rest and ring my doorbell around 9 a.m."

The next day we had all gathered at Mr. Conti's house raring to go.

"Are we going to start nailing pieces together now?" Danny asked. Danny liked to hammer things and he wanted to be first in line to start hammering.

"Not yet Danny. The first thing you need to learn about is how you build a frame. Frames are the key to building sturdy walls and roofs. Let's go look at my shed and see what I did and if there are any ideas you guys can apply to your fort."

The five of us walked over to his shed, opened the door, and walked in, not sure where to look or what to do.

Mr. Conti started, "You see boys, to make things sturdy, you need to build a strong frame. Look at my walls and see how the 2 x 4s form a box. Can you also see that there are 2 x 4s in between the big box? This is what makes the wall sturdy. The same goes for the roof."

"So if we build a frame for our roof using the leftover 2 x 4s, it should be sturdy enough?" Timmy asked.

"Probably, Tim," Mr. Conti answered. "But there are a bunch more things to figure out. Do any of you guys have any idea of what else we need to know?"

We all sat there wondering where this was going. I know Danny wanted to start nailing wood together and the rest of us were just as anxious to finish the fort so we could enjoy the two-plus days of effort we had put in already. At this juncture, I think Mr. Conti read my mind.

"You guys have done a great job so far. You have made a plan, you went out and dug a great foundation, and gathered a bunch of wood. You worked your butts off to get where you are today. I know you want to go enjoy your fort but you told me you wanted a great roof, not a quick roof. I think we can get a great roof ready to go in about an hour or two at the most. I am confident you all can be sitting in your fort after lunch if we can all stay focused."

"Why don't you guys go over and play some horseshoes and think about what you want to do. As a group you should decide whether to do the quick roof or the sturdy roof. This is your fort — I am OK with either answer," Mr. Conti said as he gave us a big smile and walked back into his house.

Danny was the first to speak, "Let's go. I am bored and want to finish the fort right now. Plus, I have a family picnic at my cousin Steven's I need to go to in a couple hours anyway. This is already more than I wanted to do."

Timmy was the quiet one but the guy who got us started down this path with his inspirational speech about building a real roof.

He leaned in: "I want to do this the right way and build something we can use regardless of the weather. I want something that says we kick ass." We all giggled a little as he said "ass. " "Danny, do what you need to do, but I am staying and am going to learn how to frame our roof," Timmy added.

Jimmy and I really had no choice. We were the ones who got this thing rolling in the first place. And we are the guys who got Mr. Conti involved, which was going to serve us well if we stuck to it. I loved having Danny involved as he had brought the hammer and nails from his Dad, along with his typical goofiness. But he had a family outing and I REALLY wanted to build a cool fort.

"I am with Timmy on this one. I want to stick around," I whispered. "How about you, Jimmy?"

Jimmy didn't hesitate a bit. "I am going to stay as well," he shared loudly, almost making a statement.

Danny nodded, as he understood what we wanted

to do and turned to walk home. "I will need my Dad's hammer. Can one of you drop it off at the house when you are done?"

"I got it Danny," I said. "I will put it on the back step of your house before you get home from your picnic." And with that he was gone.

The fort-building team was now a threesome.

With Danny's departure, Mr. Conti returned to our group with some string.

"What's that for?" Timmy asked.

"Well Tim, we can't build a frame for your roof if we don't know how big it's supposed to be, right?" Timmy nodded. "I figured that you can measure the distance from the back wall to the front of the fort with this string by either marking the string or cutting it off at the right distance. You should do the same from the sidewall to the other sidewall. Make sure the walls are standing straight when you mark that second distance. Any questions?"

"None here," Jimmy shouted.

"What's in your hand, Mr. Conti?" Timmy asked.

"That's a pocket knife, Tim," he replied. "I was wondering if you wanted to use it to cut the string at the right distance. I need to know that I can trust you with this knife and that you know the importance of using it safely."

None of us had ever used a knife before. This felt like a big deal. I am pretty sure my Mom would not have let us use our Dad's pocketknife by ourselves. Mr. Conti stood there with a look that was one part serious and one part what-are-you-going-to-do smirk. It was hard to figure out but one thing was for sure—Timmy was going to use that knife.

"Mr. Conti," Timmy said, "you can trust me with the knife. I will keep it with me and only use it to cut the two string pieces for the roof. We can be back here in 20 minutes or less," he added.

"That's great, Tim," Mr. Conti said. "But I would like to show you two simple rules for using my knife, or any knife for that matter. First, always cut away from your body like this."

With that he took the string, marked a distance with his thumb on the string, and then put the knife at that place. He then pulled his hands back from that cutting point and pushed the knife away from his body into the air.

"See how the knife went through the string and then into the air instead of against my leg or into my hand?"

We all nodded.

Mr. Conti continued. "Second rule—and this one is one of my biggies—whenever you are not using the knife, you should always fold it back into its case using the dull side of the knife and the palm of your hand. Watch this."

And with that he very simply closed the knife, and the sharp blade folded back into its case.

Mr. Conti handed Timmy the knife and off we went to measure out the two dimensions of the roof for our fort. It took no more than 10 minutes to get up the hill, measure out the two dimensions, cut the string, and return to Mr. Conti's back yard.

"Good job, boys," Mr. Conti said with enthusiasm. Timmy handed him his knife back. "Now we need to build a frame."

In total we needed to build a frame that was basically 8 x 6 feet.

"Let's lay out all of our 2 x 4s and see if we can find four that fit our string length," he asked us.

We laid out the two pieces of string so that they ran perpendicular to each piece forming one corner of the roof. We found two studs that were 8 feet long and we placed them on either side of the one string and then found two more studs that were shorter but still longer than our second string and placed them on the ground, forming a loose box.

"Why don't we find another three studs that are longer than the 6-foot string, guys? These will serve as the in-between pieces just like my wall in the shed. Remember when I said that those in-between studs give the wall or your roof the sturdiness that Tim wants," Mr. Conti instructed.

With that we laid out the frame, where we had two perfectly sized 8-foot sides and five not-so-perfect studs of differing lengths.

"Looks like we have a problem," Timmy said to no one in particular. "What do we do now?"

We were all gathered around the frame sitting on the ground staring at the mostly organized soon-to-be frame for our roof.

Mr. Conti said, "The way I see it, we can spend

some time cutting each of those 2 x 4s to be the right size like I did with the wall in my shed. Or, we can make it so they each hang over the basic square frame kind of like an awning. The first one looks clean but takes more time to make all those cuts. The second option is quicker but looks a little weird. It all depends on what you want. I am going to run inside and go to the bathroom while you guys decide."

For the second time today we were faced with a big decision. A decision we needed to make amongst the team with no help from Mr. Conti again.

Jimmy spoke first this time, "I think we should do the second option of no cuts. It's not a cop out, I just like the idea of having something that looks . . . different. If we let those studs hang over the main box frame, we could do some pretty cool things. The saved time does not stink either."

Timmy looked to me for my thoughts. "I like Jimmy's idea too."

"Let's do it!" I exclaimed.

Mr. Conti returned to the back lawn where we were sitting.

"OK boys, second big decision of the day, how do you want to proceed?"

I started the conversation for us. "We all want to build the easy frame that needs no cuts, not to save time, but to have a roof that is unique. Jimmy has some ideas of what we can do with the studs sticking out the front of the fort. Is that OK with you?"

"Of course it is, Chris," Mr. Conti said, as he looked me in the eye. "This is your fort. I am only here because you asked me to help you build your fort. Let's get this framed out so you guys can get to enjoying your new fort!"

For the next hour we built a simple box outer frame as Mr. Conti showed us how to hammer the nails into the ends of the stud. Next we laid the extra studs on top of the frame nailing each to the top of the frame at both the bottom and the top, making sure we were flush on the bottom and the overhang of each stud was on the top. We needed just three lengths of 2 x 4s to cover the entire box. In the end, we had a very sturdy roof frame.

Next up, we needed to place the pieces of plywood on the frame to complete the roof. We started placing each individual piece on the frame like a puzzle, trying to find the right combination so that each piece would create a solid 8 x 6 foot roof.

After about 10 minutes, it became apparent that we did not have enough plywood for complete coverage.

At this point, Jimmy and I looked at each other and knew what the other was thinking. This whole thing started when we spotted a large piece of plywood leaning up against Mr. Conti's shed. That piece would be perfect.

"Ummm . . . I was thinking . . . Ummm," I kind of mumbled to no one in particular.

"What is it Chris?" Mr. Conti asked.

"It does not look like we have enough plywood to cover the entire roof. Jimmy and I were wondering if you could give us that piece over there leaning against the shed," I said somewhat reluctantly. It was a gutsy move by my 10-year-old self, but we had come all this way and I was not about to stop now.

Jimmy jumped in, "We don't have any money, but maybe we could do a few chores for you as like payment or something."

"That's a good idea, Jim and Chris. I appreciate you asking me. That took a lot of guts for you I am sure. Let's grab that piece and bring it over and see how it fits first," Mr. Conti said.

Of course it fit almost perfectly as the length was exactly 8 feet and the width was exactly 4 feet. That piece combined with the other pieces formed an even 6 x 8 foot roof. And, we had our little overhang of the 2 x 4s just as Jimmy had imagined.

We proceeded to nail the plywood to our frame and with that, we had ourselves a roof for the best fort we had ever built. The three of us struggled, but we carried that frame through the houses and up the hill to the fort. Believe me, it was really heavy with all those 2 x 4s and the plywood. We placed the frame on the back of the hill near our back wall and slid it down until it was sitting on the two sidewalls we had built the day before. The sidewalls slid right up under the roof frame and we simply nailed the roof to the 2 x 4s at the top of the walls.

Once that was in place, Timmy put the tarp on top of the roof, securing it with some extra string to the studs all the way around the outside of the fort. Jimmy and I placed some small rocks, the extra dirt and some leaves on top of the tarp, which created almost a camouflage bunker-type of look. The fort was very very cool looking indeed.

When we were done, we raced back down the hill and ran over to Mr. Conti's and told him that the fort was essentially done. Mrs. Conti served us lunch that day as we all rambled on about how we had just built the best fort we had ever built. Each of us had smiles from ear to ear as we had definitely moved up a class level in our fort building.

After lunch we returned to the fort and just lay there admiring our work. In less than three days, we had built a very sturdy fort that would stand for at least two years before we took it apart to build a bigger fort.

But that story is for another day.

Fort Building

The fort-building story is a simple parable that is rich with lessons to apply to your own startup journey. Startups are hard. I trust that we all know that by now. We know most startups will fail at some point, most probably within 12–18 months of the decision to launch. Intellectually there is a healthy portion of our brains that have read, heard, and processed those facts.

Yet by definition we entrepreneurs are optimistic about our ideas. In another side of our brain, we have ruminated, poked-n-pulled, and massaged this idea for a very long time. We have completed some amount of online research on customers or partners or vendors. We have made visits both virtual and physical to entities that will be important for our idea to take hold. And we have fulfilled the dream by creating a name, a logo, and a brand for our brilliant idea.

Like any good movie thriller pitting good versus evil, these two sides of our brain create an obvious natural internal tension. This tension is at the core of your decision to make the proverbial leap.

For some, this tension prevents many would-be entrepreneurs from making the launch decision. For those who make the leap, some get bogged down by creating too much complexity early on and basically never get out of the starting gate.

So, how does one then manage that tension?

I have used the idea of fort building for many years. By definition, the parable is designed so that each one of you can easily consume and react to the messages within the story. And, as my business partner likes to say, "Chris's story has the added benefit of being true."

All of the characters in my fort-building parable are real people. I built lots of forts with these guys as a kid. As an adult, I have not stopped building forts—I have only found new fort builders on my journey.

There are five basic areas of fort building, which are closely aligned with creating a startup company. Jimmy and I learned, and now you will learn, to:

1 Socialize the Idea without Fear or Inhibition
2 Partner with Skilled and Trustworthy People
3 Gather the Assets Closest to You
4 Create a Short-Term Collective Purpose
5 Build the Fort

Let's get started and see where the lessons learned from Jimmy's and my fort-building experience can help you in your startup journey.

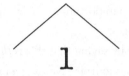

1
Socialize the Idea without Fear or Inhibition

When I think about building the fort, I think about the thing that kick-started us: "Hey Chrissy, want to build a fort?" Jimmy asked.

This was a very simple and direct question. Jimmy delivered it without agenda, peer pressure, fear, or angst. Let's think about it—what 10-year-old is afraid of an idea? In Jimmy's mind, any answer of mine was acceptable.

But Jimmy did something very important in that simple little question. What Jimmy did was **socialize his idea**. This is one of the strongest pieces of advice I give to budding entrepreneurs every day.

An idea that never makes the light of day will forever remain an idea that never has a chance of becoming something special. Believe me, I don't socialize every one of my ideas. Some stay inside my head rattling around for days or weeks, waiting for an exit. Most fade away and die out. But the important ones make it out into the sunlight. Bringing your idea out of your head is the first step on your startup journey.

Why is this so important and why should you share your idea with others?

Let me start by saying that this is *the* most important stage of your startup journey. No exaggeration or hyperbole here. I am not aware of one business that exists solely inside your own head. Even solo inventors have to tell/show someone their invention at some point, right?

Are you ready to take this idea to the outside world? Please say yes.

Let's start with all the reasons why you should socialize your idea even at its most raw, most vulnerable stage.

Newsbreak: your idea is probably not novel. There are at least 10 people somewhere thinking the same exact thing you are. If it is not exactly the same thing, it is close enough that any buyer would not discriminate when making a purchasing decision between their product and yours. And even if there are other products all competing for the same dollar, you may be up against some incumbent business that everyone is already comfortable with.

Most of us start by conceiving a product that meets a personal need. It is a great place to start. It is the first match that lights our fire and ignites some dormant passion of ours. Fantastic.

But you are just one customer. You need many others and every one of them will have a different idea of what this product is and how it should work.

For the past days/weeks/months you have been thinking about colors, logos, features, and the smiles on the faces of many future customers. But what if I told you that over half the features you are thinking about would never be used yet paid for, and that the manner in which customers interact with your product will create too much friction for most, if not all, of your intended users?

These issues are all game enders. Most startups run out of time and money before they discover their product and market. Too many times I see talented entrepreneurs who have worked tirelessly perfecting a product inside their own heads or even in their basements before they bring it out to the world. Sometimes months of effort and hundreds of thousands of dollars later, they emerge to show the world their brilliant creation. Then the world votes with its disinterest. What a waste of time and effort.

Steve Blank, noted author and blogger who teaches entrepreneurship at University of California–Berkeley's Haas Business School, Columbia University, NYU, Stanford University Engineering School, and UCSF—and developed the concept of Customer Development, the precursor to the Lean Startup movement—has a great quote: "No business plan ever survives the first contact with a customer." You can insert "product" for "business plan" and "friend/colleague/wife/husband/parent/neighbor" for "customer," and the statement still holds true.

Let me share with you my first CEO hint: your job is to find the most productive and efficient path to success for your product and business. Very few of you if any have all the answers for your product, sales, and operations of your business.

Socialize your idea now. The result will be a better, more well-rounded concept that will start to stand up to early scrutiny. Every minute and dollar working on the wrong element of your business is wasted and pulling you away from success.

Thinking back, when Jimmy pitched me the idea of building a fort that day, he obviously had some thoughts about its location, size, and what it might look like when we finished. He had been working on this idea in his head for some time. Remember that he wanted an upgraded fort that held more people and had a real roof that blocked the rain from getting in.

For the first 10–20 minutes of that conversation we just discussed what the fort could be. This is my favorite part of the journey. Why? At this stage, it's all about the dream and nothing can stand in the way of the obviously successful outcome. In order for Jimmy's dream to come true he had to share it with someone. It was the first test of his dream.

This is where channeling your inner 10-year-old is critical. How many of you are afraid to share your idea with someone with the notion that your idea is too raw? This is an adult affect that begins building early in our life. I hate it, too. We have to eliminate this from our early journey. It is an inhibitor, hands down.

As I mentioned earlier, there are probably 10 people already working on a version of what you are thinking about.

Worried? You should be. But don't let that stop you from socializing your idea. Because here is the dirty little secret—it's not the idea, it's the execution of the idea that will mean more to the success of the business in the long run. So if it's not the idea, then there should be no reason to share the idea with others, right?

Don't get me wrong, your spin on something may be very unique and even something special that customers might gravitate to. But you still need to build it out and show it to people. How are you going to do that alone? You need to socialize your idea without fear of anyone stealing it.

The good news is that you have been thinking about this a lot longer than anyone else has. To that end, you have somewhat of an advantage. Now go do it faster and better than everyone else.

■

Your first conversation should be with the person closest to you. This should be your spouse, partner, or significant other. Maybe this is a sibling or a parent. It could be a former boss or peer in the business you are working at today.

This journey will be rocky. If you have a partner, they will live most of what you are living right along with you. You need some buy-in from them. Not permission per se, but buy-in is tantamount to a lasting relationship. Bring them into your idea early. Just simply share what you are thinking. And why not—they are the safest person you know in the world. They should not judge—they should support. It's why you picked them to be the first person to hear your idea.

You can set a couple different expectations for this discussion. (1) You can ask them just to listen and allow you the time and space to get this out of your head and into the world. For most of us, this is a critical psychological step. Pushing your idea out into the world gives the idea a life beyond just you. With a first listener, their reaction(s) can be the first test of whether this even makes sense. (2) You can ask the listener to ask you three to five questions. Those first, typically higher-level questions are the first indicators to the holes in your thinking.

One of my favorite questions for a budding startup founder is, "Who have you talked to about this? Why?"

I need to know how serious you are about pursuing the idea. If you can't socialize the idea, you are already in a heap of trouble. You see, the startup journey will be littered with self-doubt, internal angst regarding important decisions, and multiple occasions of "should I go on." These moments require a safe and supportive network. Socializing your idea early on or showing me you can socialize your idea at its rawest stage is an indicator that you will also rely on the network when things get invariably tough.

There is one more aspect to your first socializing that is subtle but pretty important. Your first outline of your idea will probably be pretty bad. Your excitement will override your need to be short and concise and your "pitch" will be all over the place. Don't despair; there are easy ways to improve upon this. The first is practice. The more you do it, the better it should get. Your first handful of pitches will meander around looking for a purpose. The people across the table from you will ask certain questions that highlight the deficiencies in your talk track. Listen to them and modify accordingly. Each socializing opportunity is a chance to hone your words. Each interaction serves as little nugget of gold.

Building a fort is a lot of fun—for about a day or two. As 10-year-olds we only had so much patience and attention span. The early socializing between Jimmy and me was a test of some sort. Jimmy was looking for validation that the idea was not crazy. I gave that to him. But I also started to buy in myself with a series of questions. "Where do you want to build the fort this time?" I asked. That dialogue is my favorite part of the fort-building process. Think about it; there are no rules, no constraints, and no bullshit. We were just two kids dreaming a little. Close your eyes. Can you see two kids smiling ear to ear riffing on a bunch of fort-building ideas?

The ultimate goal—after those first friendly conversations—is to find the glaring weak spots in the business. First and foremost is your rambling explanation of the idea. Let's face it; you are doing a pretty bad job of explaining the business concept. Your mother, friend, or best friend will give you plenty of room to get there — professional peers and investors will not.

Time and time again, I see this from first-time founders. Its not a deal breaker but you have to fix it. I can't help you if you can't explain it in a simple, meaningful way.

Some of you have heard the line, "Explain it like you are explaining it to your grandmother." It's not just a cliché. Overwhelming me with detail before I have a chance to understand the big picture works against you. If you think fire hosing me in order to show me how smart you are will impress me, you are completely wrong. I promise you I — and everyone else — will be more impressed with a simple and concise version of your idea.

After first sharing with close friends, go find two or three others. Why? Each version gets a little different as you react to your new friends on the other side of the coffee table. Three very positive things start to happen with repetition:

1 You get better at explaining complex areas of your idea.

2 You gain a little confidence as you see instant positive feedback that they get it.

3 You start to think about your idea through their eyes instead of just yours.

Years ago, business building was very linear. First, you conceived an idea, which resulted in some type of prototype. Then you identified a manufacturer that could mass produce said product. Then you went and found distributors to partner with or you went direct and hired sales people to push your product into various channels.

Once the product hit the shelves, you then opened up the sales funnel by expanding into more channels or widened the product line with additional product versions or concepts. Each subsequent move built upon the previous success gate.

For most products, this required a healthy and early capital infusion coupled with a staff of experienced operators to hit each milestone. And each milestone was measured in multiple months to a year, a long timeline indeed, but no more.

Remember that first, there are many tools available to expedite certain milestones. Second, these tools enable first-time founders to operate "with experience." Third, these two elements conspire together to minimize the capital needs.

The result is a nonlinear, more circular approach to business building. The first step is the feedback loop.

So whom might you test this out on?

■

My favorite next step is to get your idea in front of some people who may be customers of your product or service. Customers? But I don't have a product and I don't know how I am going to price it or deliver it and I don't even have a logo yet! Relax, Francis (insert *Stripes* movie reference here). Right here — in this moment — is where you need to rewire your brain. Your thinking is totally wrong. Here's why.

One job as CEO/founder is to validate as quickly and cheaply as possible whether there is a business here or not. Quickly and cheaply! Finding out six months later after you have quit your job would be a bad time to hear from potential customers that your product is not needed. Or, more important, that the way you are planning on implementing the product/service is DOA (dead on arrival). Many a good product idea dies from customers confused over how they will buy the product or service.

The days of building the entire product and then going out to sell it are over. This is not a linear process anymore. Today, we operate in a continual series of feedback loops that hone our product or service to the needs of our targeted customer set.

After getting some initial buy in from your spouse, good friend, or dad, you will approach these seasoned targets. Who are they? We have now moved into phase two of the socializing step and are migrating from the safe pitch to the professional pitch.

Now don't freak out and overthink this; you are simply trying to ramp up the feedback quality a notch or three.

The second round of socializing your idea (aka the professional feedback phase) is pretty scary for some people. When you break it down to its core elements, you are going to a complete stranger and exposing your deepest darkest secret—the secret being that you have an idea that is half-baked and maybe half-stupid.

Like the preparation you do for any important meeting, you need to have a goal in mind. Your startup concept is fraught with assumptions yet to be validated, so you have one overarching goal: test your hypothesis with people who are in or around your idea.

Who might these people be and whom do they represent?

The first one on my list would be potential customers. At the end of the day, if no one buys, there is no business. If you are a business software concept directed at the HR department of midsize banks, go find a few HR directors.

If you are a social photo-sharing site targeted at 40-year-old hockey players, go find an ice rink at 10 p.m. any night and talk to some old hockey players. (I'll see you there—I will be the old guy.)

The sooner we get our ideas in front of customers, the sooner we can determine what the product should do and how they want to consume that product.

Finally, here is one tip that should provide comfort: at this stage you are not selling them anything—you are simply interviewing them and getting their feedback. There is no pressure in that course of action.

So, get out there and start talking to customers now.

■

The next group of professionals I want to talk to early in my process are those associated with the cost or building of my product.

For a software product, it is the software developers. For a medical device, it might be the hardware manufacturers. You get the idea. If you are opening a retail store, it will be the product manufacturers. If you are building a brick-and-mortar store, add landlords to that list too. Our goal here is to get some very preliminary ideas as to how difficult it would be to build out your product. We are talking about rough order of magnitude here.

The simplest of business principles are in question here: Can I ultimately sell this for more than it takes me to create it? Sounds funny, right? I am not talking about prototypes or beta software. Think at a higher level than that. But start thinking about this equation early on and ask a few experts their opinion about the level of effort that would be required.

Again, many a business fails when they find out that the costs to acquire, convert, and maintain a customer is more than the revenue generated by that same customer.

Next on my list would be people who are experienced in selling the product. These can be direct selling agents (sales people) or marketing agents (if this is a product that will be consumed from the Internet without a sales person to facilitate the transaction).

Good news here: they like to talk, so wind them up, sit back, and soak it all in. Ask them how they find their customers and how much it costs per paid customer. Ask them how much time it takes to identify, sell, and close a sale (aka the sales cycle.) Ask them what the most frequent objections are to a customer purchase. Finally, ask them what one thing they would do differently than they are doing today to create more sales. Why? As a startup, you need to find great thinkers, not just salesmen. Maybe you'll find both sensibilities in the same head. That's good.

A couple things are going on here that are important to talk about now.

The world is littered with decent products that never find a customer, from the bar down the street that you love and is always empty to those 500 perfectly designed toilet-paper-cover contraptions that sit in your garage. In my software world, I can't tell you how many products/apps are out there searching for a customer to find them. There are 1.5 million apps in the Apple App store as of July 2015—1.5 million is a lot of noise to work through just to get someone to see your app.

It is not enough just to build the product. Someone has to sell it. A business with product and no sales is not a business. We refer to this as the "Field of Dreams" strategy as in "Build It and They Will Come." Turns out they won't.

Use these early discussions with sales and marketing

people as the first indicators of how you might get your product sold. This is more important than the product. The really cool part is that some of these people might be a few of your first hires when you get the business up and running. Again, don't sell them—just ask them a lot of questions. No fear.

So, in our professionally focused feedback tour we listed customers, cost providers, and sales and marketing agents as resources. Who else could we talk to? If the idea is a business you used to be in, then I would talk to former coworkers, peers, bosses, competitors, and clients. Tread a little carefully here and use good judgment in how you represent yourself. Don't lie. Be a good citizen.

The task is for you to reach out and meet with 20+ people—some of whom you have never met before. (You said you wanted to be a CEO and build a great company, right? Well guys/gals—this is where you separate the wannabe's from the real McCoys. How is that for a mixed metaphor?)

So, how does one get this socialization tour started? Well, your Uncle Chris is here to help. There are two basic tasks in front of you now: figuring out (1) how to find these people, and (2) how to convince them to take your meeting. Remember, your task as CEO is to garner the resources necessary to execute on your vision. Consider these next meetings as a set of resources.

At the ripe old age of 42, I had built a career that labeled me as an Internet General Manager. By General

Manager, I mean that I had full P&L responsibility. Think of a GM as the CEO of a business unit or division within a larger company. Things were looking good except for the fact that this was right after the dot.com bomb in 2001. I could not find a GM job doing anything related to the Internet.

Then Gail Meneley appeared in my life. While helping out an old friend, I met Gail and her partner, who had the premier executive outplacement firm in Chicago. Think C-suite executives who need some help determining what comes next in their lives. I was working from a home office consulting for a small software company and Gail asked me to bring my youthful energy to their offices. Under the adage "It is never too late to learn a new skill," I learned how to network effectively under their tutelage. Here's what I learned about effective networking, which I boiled down to four simple segments:

1 Have a compelling story

2 Share without fear what you need to take this to the next step

3 Ask for three introductions to like-minded people, and

4 End with this simple question, "What can I do for you?"

A story is a pitch without "the ask" built in. People respond to a story. A story has a little emotion in it. A story targets your heart as well as your brain. Tell a story. Don't make it up — make it real. Why are you pursuing this idea? Why are you going to make this happen? Share the feedback from a few of the prior conversations. Tell a story.

When you get to the end of the story, share what you need to go forward. If your listeners are potential customers, tell them you need to understand the customer need and the potential value of your product in their lives. If you are looking to raise investment capital, ask them if they know anyone who would be interested in this type of investment. Regardless of what you need, ask for three names from them. It goes as simply as this, "Who else should I be sharing this story with?"

Lastly, finish with a simple question: "Is there anything I can do for you?" And mean it. You can make introductions as well. You can volunteer for their next event. You can follow them on Twitter or subscribe to their blog. Do something, regardless of how small. It shows up on the scorecard.

There are two little secrets that great networkers live by, the warm introduction and the follow up. Warm introductions trump cold emails or calls every day. The difference between the two is measured in miles. Your job is to get a warm intro from the person you just met with the three people they committed to introduce you to. No wiggle room here. Get the commitment from them. That being said, the ball is in your court regardless of what was said.

Yes, in the meeting I indicated that I would introduce you to three people. Now, I want you to email me after our meeting and remind me of the three people. Your follow up does two things, (1) you tell me that you are serious and you are willing to pull your weight in this, and (2) it triggers me to act.

At its core, networking is a pay-it-forward exercise. Give and you will get. Thanks, Gail for a new skill. I couldn't have mastered it without you.

I also want you to think like a 10-year-old with no fear or inhibition. Build the fort! And make a list. Mine will be a spreadsheet with each tab representing each of the categories of people I want to talk to (customers, investors, cost providers, sales and marketing, etc.). I will work my personal custom spider web for each category. A systematic methodology is my key to success.

■

By now you may be wondering why anyone you don't know would take a meeting with you. Can you feel the doubt creep in? It's a little fear that needs to be put down now. Right now—right here I am going to dispel this fear. Ready?

Your story is worthwhile and people want to hear it. Let me repeat this, PEOPLE WANT TO HEAR YOUR STORY! Why? There may be something in it for them.

Remember the pay-it-forward mentality? You are going to do something for them. This is a two-way deal. If you approach it that way, the feeling that you have to convince them that there is reason to meet with you fades away.

I believe that most of us want to help others succeed. It is certainly true for entrepreneurs, whose DNA has a built-in giveback component. In fact that is my litmus test for whether you are a true entrepreneur. If you ask what's in it for you—you are not an entrepreneur. The best founders have created their success on the backs of hundreds of mentors, advisors, investors, employees, and customers, all who participated in the feedback loop. They will take your meeting!

Listen, at its most fundamental level, you have to totally, 100%, no-holds-barred, believe in your idea. If you truly believe that, won't others want to hear about it too? If you network into the right people through warm introductions, and if you can tell a simple yet compelling story, and if you can muscle through a few early versions of your pitch that evolve into a great pitch—people will respond. I promise. Those who don't respond won't matter anyway. You have to kiss a few frogs to get to your princes.

Ready to start? One more thought.

Are you worried that someone might steal your idea? It is brilliant, is it not? This is where some of you clutch and do something really stupid.

Some of you might be thinking OK, I will socialize this but I will either protect my idea with some legal document or tell a watered-down, vanilla version of my pitch. This makes perfect sense to you. The argument in your head goes like this — I am smart, I have dreamed this up, I own this brilliant thinking, I need to protect it, it is my asset.

The NDA (non-disclosure agreement) is a typical corporate form and easy to obtain even without a lawyer. The NDA basically says, everything we talk about is confidential and you can't talk about this for one, three, or five years without notifying me. So you pop this paper document in front of your new friend and ask her to sign it.

Congratulations — you have just eliminated 80% of the people you should talk to, because they won't sign it. Even worse, the 20% who did sign it are idiots and you don't want them anyhow. Why?

You want to bring your idea to the best startup people around. These guys and gals have waded through the startup trenches. They have the scars from building companies themselves. Their role in your journey is to ask perfect questions that sharpen your idea. They also will recommend the next set of people to talk to. It's what they do. Trust me.

The best advisors/mentors meet people like you every day. Imagine if they signed a NDA document for every person who came to see them. Think how limiting and onerous that would be to manage. Remember, you are not unique — you are one of a hundred just this year. Skip the NDA and trust the system.

I find that socializing your idea is the most rewarding step in the startup process. Why? You get to share your deepest thoughts without actually having to do anything but talk. The best ideas and companies come from an amalgamation of different viewpoints and opinions. Go get as many of those as you can. I promise you it will make your idea that much better. Isn't that what you want? Don't you want to create a great business? First-time entrepreneurs sometimes get caught in the trap of thinking that exposing the idea is risky. It's exactly the opposite.

Got you convinced yet? I hope so.

■

I have been involved with at least 15 of my own startups and have invested in about 50 more. At this point in my life, I have seen some serious patterns emerge that are worth sharing.

I have sat in an upstairs office in my house and drafted some of the most exquisite business plans ever. Ever. Perfectly formatted words with just the right amount of colorful graphs were generated to highlight the depth of my thinking. And then . . . nothing. I was all thought—no socializing. Where was I to go from here? I did not understand the value of getting feedback. I was the smart one. Wrong.

Later in life, I tried the opposite tack, more of an all-socializing, limited-thinking attack. Looking back, I realize that fear played a large role in my approach. No feedback equals no bad news.

Today, I work hard to find people smarter than me.

On September 27th, 2009, my current employer and self-appointed-investor-turned-CEO and I sat down to lunch. He had come on board about three months prior and I was the standing COO. He had asked me to stick around to bring him up to speed. I knew what was inevitable, I just did not know when. So I continued to work hard for the company but I also began to mentally prepare for what was next.

For the previous 10–12 years, I had been the hired gun that investors parachute into an existing entity to help take the company to the next step. The dirty little secret in this path is that you are asked to leave as easily as you arrive.

On that Wednesday as we had lunch, he told me it was the end of the road for me. (By the way, no amount of mental preparation or even multiple firings help with the evil your brain will inflict upon you later; I know—this was the third time this had happened to me.) That being said, I thanked him and walked out that afternoon.

I made two calls that same afternoon with local entrepreneur types to talk about my new idea for a new-age incubator program. My first meetings were that following Friday at breakfast, 48 hours after that lunch. I did something different to get different results. I did not hunker down for a few days/weeks/months to figure things out. I jumped right back in two days later.

This startup would be different. I would approach this in a completely opposite manner. The Startup Factory investment/mentor business was launched that day. TSF has many components but two critical ones revolve around people, namely, entrepreneurs and mentors. In this startup, I soon realized I would need to acquire plenty of both. So I started socializing my idea. Six months later, I had sat one-on-one with more than 275 people.

I created personal momentum. Personal momentum is really valuable.

I love to talk about momentum. For me it is everything. Whether you are talking about personal momentum or professional momentum or business momentum—forward acceleration is good for everything. Momentum creates a sense of purpose and builds on itself. It is an unbelievable feeling to be in the vortex of a momentum-driven journey. Socializing your idea with 10–20 really smart, opinionated peers creates momentum. This is why I love the socialization part of a startup so much. When you do it right, each meeting builds on the prior meeting. Each interaction is an opportunity to make every aspect of the idea better. The best part is that as you grab the energy from each one of those meetings, your body produces chemicals that in fact create more energy for you.

It's like a free and legal form of entrepreneurial cocaine without any of the downside.

There is a great personal by-product of the momentum ride for me that is really important: confidence. For me, each meeting gives me a little more confidence that I know what the heck I am doing. Each meeting enables me to quiet the internal critics that so love to show their face. If for no other reason than some sort of personal confidence machine, build some momentum through your idea socializing.

When building the fort as 10-year-olds, Jimmy and I had our initial discussion with a typical 10-year-old's pure perspective. There was no risk of either one of us thinking this was stupid. We used each other to build a confidence that we could pull this off, and neither one of us brought any emotional baggage. We trusted each other as kids do. We had no fear that either one of us would make the other feel inferior. Ten-year-olds don't have that motor yet. It comes later, I guess.

■

The decision to start something on your own is a total mind blower. If it isn't scary for you, it should be. Making the decision to kick off a business starts hard and then gets harder. The feeling is even worse if this is your first time. It's OK; we have all been through it. It's not unnatural and you are not unique. If this decision doesn't make you sweat a little you may be a delusional sociopath.

Why fear though?

Let's take a stroll down Maslow's hierarchy and see what we come up with.

At our most basic human level, we need to take care of our physiological needs, including food and water. As we move up the pyramid, we are then motivated by safety (security of home, employment, health and body). Unless we are independently wealthy, we have a very basic need to provide for ourselves and potentially our family. How are we going to live?

Marc Cuban slept on his buddy's couch after college. Many in their 30s have moved back in with their parents. Some take crappy off-hour jobs simply to cover their expenses and give them time to work their idea during the day. We do what we have to do to cover our basic human needs. Cross-tab these needs with the doubts you have about the efficacy of your idea and that is enough to create a healthy chunk of good old-fashioned fear.

The idea of covering your basic needs is simple enough, right? Wrong. The question that crops up is, What is "basic"? One man's ramen noodle is another man's Ruth's Chris, I guess. I can't tell you how many times I hear a wannabe entrepreneur share with me that if only they could get investment dollars they would quit their job. Then they drive off in their Mercedes Benz. For me, this is what separates the entrepreneurial men/women from the boys/girls. As an investor I want to see — in action, not words — that you are 100% committed to growing the business. That commitment comes in many forms but the first one is the financial level you are willing to live on. Or better put, sacrifice to. As an investor I want to see that you need to make this idea work at any cost.

What can you do to prepare yourself for the leap? Get your financial house in order and plan for at least a 12–18 month run. Are you a recent college grad? Move back in with Mom and Dad or beg one of your buddies to sleep on her couch until she kicks you out. Then find another buddy.

Are you in your late 20s and have you been working for The Man for the last six years? Cut way back on your expenses for 6–12 months leading up to your leap and build up a financial cushion to support your leap. Are you a 40-something former executive making a healthy six figures with a mortgage, car payment, and kids in private school? Swap your luxury car for a used sedan, scale back the trips to Cabo, and move the kids into public school (oh the horror). Like the late 20s guy, begin to pack away some extra finances leading up to your leap to financially support your run.

The important thing to remember is this: your risk should at least be commensurate to my investor risk. If I am risking my investment dollars and you are not risking your lifestyle at all, the equation is not balanced and the only person who will invest is your mother. I don't love you like she does. I never will.

If you are not planning on taking on investors I am happy for you. You just simplified your life considerably. However, the financial issue remains. Do you have 12–18 months of personal runway packed away? Want to take financial fear out of the equation? Plan for it.

What else causes fear? How about, "I don't know if this idea is any good." It's a classic and I would add a pretty good fear as fear goes. Let me give you a hint—your idea probably sucks. At least the current version of your idea. Welcome to the startup club where ideas come and go like taxis in New York City.

There is a basic premise we talk about with all of our investments at The Startup Factory and it goes like this. At least 10 other groups are working on your idea or a reasonably close version of your idea somewhere in the world. Knowing this, does that make you stop moving ahead with your idea? Does this form a huge boulder in your stomach? The execution of your idea is the most important factor, and managing your fear is one of the more critical elements in successful execution.

Over the past few years a ton has been written with regard to testing your startup hypotheses. Executed correctly, these new methodologies will deliver to you really healthy indications on the possible success of your idea. Sometimes even before you make the leap.

I don't need to go into huge detail here but Eric Reis's *The Lean Startup*, *Nail It Then Scale It* from Nathan Furr and Paul Ahlstrom, and Steve Blank's *Four Steps to the Epiphany* (and his outstanding blog at www.steveblank.com) are must-reads. It took me a few months to a year to exorcise all my traditional/dated software-founder business-building thoughts before these books entered my soul. Now, The Startup Factory is 100% built around their thesis —that you can test and iterate yourself to a higher probability of business success, thus reducing your fear.

The close cousin of the "I don't know if this idea is any good" mind trap is the "I don't have any good ideas" thread. There are two pieces to this that need to be discussed. The first is related to the previous talk track, how do you even know what is good right now? You don't. So take the burden of determining whether this idea is good off your shoulders and move forward. Follow the best practices of today's startup gurus and run some basic tests with the targeted marketplace to determine the initial quality of your idea.

The second aspect of your fear is whether you actually have ideas that excite you.

Are you in love with the idea of being an entrepreneur? I think you are an entrepreneur when you see a business idea you just have to fix. The obsession drives you until there is no choice but to take a crack at it. If you don't have that drive toward something specific, I am not sure you are ready to be an entrepreneur.

If this feels like you, then take my advice—move on with the idea of being an entrepreneur. Go find a startup that needs someone like you and get paid to learn what it is like. Try on "the suit" I advise and see what happens. The best training ground if you are not ready is to be employee number 3–10. You get to be part of every decision without the burden of it being your baby. The exposure is priceless.

Then find or wait for an idea that excites you.

One of my favorite fear factors usually shows up with the more analytical personalities out there. Are you the kind of person who hits the Internet every time you have a notion about something so that you can find some statistics to back up your premise? In a previous life, were you an active reader of Gartner, IDC, or Forrester reports? Do you subscribe to newsletters that analyze in gory detail the components of a target company or industry?

There will never be enough public data available to you that moves your brain to a place where it says, "Go do this, it is a safe bet."

The basic nature of a great startup idea is that the idea finds a crack or a void that has not been addressed yet. By that very definition there will not be public data to support your thesis. Release the need to check off the public data/information requirement from your decision tree, build out your own data, and the fear should lessen.

The one fear that I know you should consider is "Am I any good at this?" I have to be honest with you — it's a biggie. For most of you there is a ton of doubt. I have struggled with this my entire life. As a first-time startup founder you have never navigated anything this personal since you tried out for the 8th grade soccer team. Zits, puberty, and peer pressure aside, that middle school public moment is nothing compared to the adult version. That job interview you went on a few months ago was pretty close, too, but the worst outcome from that was you did not get hired. "If you blow this startup leap you are forever scarred," you say to yourself. You know that inner part of you we all have will be screaming in your ear, "I told you . . . you are not ready for this." "Yes I am, " the other voice says. And back and forth it goes. (Right now you are channeling Tom Hulce in *Animal House*.)

Questions from the inner brain are evil. They are our worst enemy drudging up stuff from who knows where. And don't tell me you don't have them. It's like masturbating, either you do it or you lie about it. There are no in-betweens on this. The good news is you are not alone. The bad news is that you have to address it, and address it head on.

I can't sell.

I hate accounting.

I am not very good at managing people.

I don't like negotiating.

I am not smart enough to run my own business.

These are all valid fears and in some minds each one is a showstopper. You are correct, if your business can't sell something you don't have a business. Simple. But knowing that many of us have the same fears and have found ways to combat them should provide comfort and a starting point for your journey.

In the summer of 1998, I had wound down 77 Capital, the venture capital subsidiary of R.R. Donnelley & Sons. As part of this successful exit (in their eyes, not mine) I was given a substantial bonus and a severance package for my 10 years in the company.

Armed with time to do what I wanted, I started building out a plan to reinvent the mapping industry. At this time in my life, I had developed a number of professional skills that would serve me well. I had an investment contact list, I had seven+ years in the mapping business that included being the co-founder of MapQuest, and I knew how a venture-backed company was born and raised to a successful outcome. I was in a great position.

In my heart of hearts, I am a builder of things. I like to figure problems out, and then outline in a spreadsheet all the elements of the plan including projected profits, costs, etc. In the summer of 1989, I developed a plan to acquire one of the premier but undermanaged brands in the map industry. I spent weeks researching the market. I reached out to professional map-industry friends to get their latest insights. I created a new name for the company and designed a logo. And lastly, I determined how much money I would need to raise to make that acquisition and launch my company.

I did everything but call investors. Didn't I need money to get this off the ground? My energy and actions ground to a halt. I was paralyzed. What was I waiting for? You see, I had never made a cold call in my life. Put me in a meeting—I can run the show. As an investor at 77 Capital, founders came to me. I had the money. But reach out to people I did not already know? How do you do that?

So I called my mentor, Bart, and talked about the

plan and the costs and the capital required and then stopped.

He asked me, "What has been the investor reaction?" Hmmmm.

"I have not spoken to any investors yet."

Heart starts beating faster.

"Well, you have to call some, right?"

Right.

"OK, let's make a list and you can start with a few friendlies. Rory, Russell, and Ellen would be a great start. You know all of them so they will all gladly take your call. Ask each one who else you should talk to and go from there."

A month later, I had talked to 75 investors. Over half were cold calls generated from names and phone numbers previous targets had provided me. I promise you the first 5–10 calls were rough. I would pace back and forth in my attic office. I would literally stare at the phone as if it was evil. Please someone call me because that would mean you wanted to hear me tell my story.

What happened that unshackled me from my fear? It was simple—this was not going to happen unless I made the calls. Plain and simple. **I had no choice. I** wanted to launch this business and I wanted to be the man. Men make cold calls. Grab your things and hit the phone. And then a funny thing happened. After a few supportive calls, I got a little confidence. Within a day or two I could not wait to hit the phones. Seriously.

At the age of 39 I had just acquired a new skill and conquered a major fear.

Fear of failure is the mother of all fears. It's the big kahuna. It is in every one of us and it never goes away. Welcome to Startupland. Are you ready to tackle this? Without a doubt in my mind this is the proverbial elephant in the room. Deal with this and you might have a chance. Pretend it does not exist or push it back into those deep areas where we hide things and 9 times out of 10 you will suffer, as will your business.

Your internal response to all of those evil thoughts is, "I just won't fail—I cannot fail."

What an incredibly large burden to place on your new startup company and yourself. I cannot think of a larger professional weight sitting on your proverbial shoulders. The percentage of failure for startups is high—we all know that. And the likelihood as a first-time entrepreneur is even greater. So, why will you be different? Are you smarter than everyone else? There is no evidence to suggest a correlation between IQ and startup success. Will you work harder than others? Bullshit! We have all witnessed guys and gals who are torching both ends of the candle and still fail. Almost everyone I see is smart enough and they all work really hard.

So when you artificially place this incredible burden on yourself to "not fail" you create a significant psychological dimension into your startup decision making. Fear of future failure prevents good ideas and good founders from ever making the leap to Startupland.

If you don't get comfortable with the idea of failure as a potential outcome, I think most of you will be handcuffed to your current state in life and never make the decision to leap forward. Why would we? Our most basic human protection devices will kick in to prevent the horror of failure. "Oh the humanity!"

Just the thought of failure while I am writing this book and this section as a first-time author is making me sweat a little. Literally every blocking fear you can imagine is saying hello and whispering in my ear. "You have nothing new to say. This topic has been covered a hundred times. There are better-known startup Gods—what gives you the right to tell your story? Your writing is sophomoric. You know nothing about publishing. This is a complete waste of time. This will be a complete failure!!"

To hell with it—I am writing anyway. At the end of this book, I may be the only person who likes it. (This is kind of for my dad, anyway, who loved to read, wrote some beautiful short stories years ago, and died a few years ago). I have become comfortable with an audience of one (or two—I love you, Dad!).

I have talked about writing a book for at least 10 years now. For the better part of those years it was going to be the world's best bathroom/business book. Every insightful chapter could be consumed in the time it took to sit down and relive oneself. I would socialize the concept at parties and look for some reaction. The business/bathroom book concept is modestly humorous at best but really it turns out it was just another blocking mechanism. It wasn't until I started blogging regularly over the past couple years and my writing muscles got into shape that the possibility of writing a real book became an option in my mind.

For the past six months I socialized the idea of my writing this book with some friends. These are my professional friends who view me through their own professional lens. This is important, as my personal friends were like, "Go ahead—you should do this—it would be really cool—and you are so good at it!"

I love them but these friends don't count. I needed the professional friends and they needed something more than a "bathroom/business book" concept with no central theme other than it would be funny. Some type of fear prevented me from writing the business/bathroom book, as I could not even bring myself to writing an outline. An outline is the easiest limp-in task one can take. This book was going to fail.

My second foray into writing a book started with an inventory. I have been writing for Inc.com for over a year and I have more than 80 articles in my portfolio. I then went and took all of the blog posts that were general in nature (as opposed to about TSF or North Carolina's Research Triangle Park) and I summarized all of the titles and article topics into a spreadsheet.

(Does this sound like a data research play to you?) I hoped that by staring at the list that the new magical theme would emerge. Two months later the list still existed and no book was on the horizon.

Finding the theme to this book unlocked something for me—it unlocked my confidence enough to start an outline and share that outline with a few of my professional friends. The outline was then used in a TEDx talk I gave at Duke University. The response was positive. Now I am cooking. What if I wrote what I talked about at TED as I socialized the new concept with more people? My confidence was on a roll and once I crossed that confidence line and shared this publicly, there was only one thing left to do—start writing.

There are psychologists, startup gurus, and of course your mother, who can all attempt to help you with your future fear-of-failure handicap. I know that I have clutched at all of them.

But the most amazing thing I have learned (late in my career) is what it takes to recognize and combat my fear. I promise you that it is the single most gnarly beast preventing your success. It has stopped me in my tracks many times. Your task is to find ways to tame the beast.

2
Partner with Skilled & Trustworthy People

Finding friends at the age of 10 is pretty easy, I think. Finding a business partner anytime after the age of 20 is much harder. Trust is the issue and that is why so many 20-somethings start a business with their college or high-school buddy. There is built-in trust in those relationships.

One of the oldest debates in the startup world is whether you should have a co-founder or go solo to get started. Some investors like founding teams of only two or more. Some investors prefer clean ownership structures where each co-founder owns the same relative amount. Many investors shy away from sibling teams or married couples. I prefer to look at each case individually.

As for me, I have done the startup thing solo and

with partners, and the bottom line is that it all depends on the business and of course it depends on you. If you are contemplating making the leap and are ready to build your fort, this issue should be on your mind.

There are three factors that influence my thinking here:

1 Skills

2 Effort, and

3 Credibility.

Each startup will require a minimum amount of skills to get off the ground. If this is a software startup, someone needs to know how to write code. That seems obvious, but I am still surprised by the "business" guy that shows up in my office articulating his mobile app idea who has no real idea of how it's going to get made. Coming in to see me for investment capital so that you can go out and hire a developer is not the answer. Why?

Let me take you back to page 27 in this book. It's not your idea; it's the execution of your idea. To that end, the software developer you need to build out your idea is actually more important to the company than you are at this point. So, your decision to use a contractor or the decision to outsource the development of your gold seems kinda weak to me.

Your role is to marshal the resources necessary to get to the next phase/level/step. Thus, your analysis of what you need to get this off the ground is pretty simple. Do I have the necessary skills to execute the first phase? If not, you best find a partner or co-founder.

Too many founders operate on a vision of the company three years out when there are customers, employees, desks and chairs, and strategic decisions to make. Very few understand what steps are necessary to get to that place. You can't make decisions at this stage with an eye three years out. You can't execute Month 30 without surviving Month 3. You need to make decisions that give you permission to live another day. What resources do you need NOW to give you the credibility to get through to the next level?

What sorts of skills are necessary at this stage, and what sorts of skills can you live without for a while? There are only two categories you need to worry about right now: (1) customer development, and (2) product development. The prioritization is in that order too. Everything else can wait. Don't recruit your CFO. That can wait about three years—if you are lucky and good.

As I outlined in the "socialize your idea" phase, understanding the needs of your customer is paramount to building a great company. So, who is going to serve that role? Does the very thought of cold-calling someone make you run to the bathroom and hide in fear? Don't freak out yet, maybe you can find another way. Is your idea one where future customers will find you on the web, download your app, and never connect with you on the phone or in person? (I will still argue that you still need to talk to your potential customer, by the way.) Well, maybe you can get away with hiding on your computer for a little while. If that is the case, you best be able to understand how to find and engage online customers early on so that you can get that feedback loop going.

Customer development skills are a critical aspect of the company. Most of us with a builder orientation ignore or minimize the customer parts of our business. Someone else will grab my product when it's done and they will spin their magic selling skills and all will be good in "fill-in-my-company-name" fairyland.

I am a natural extrovert. Put me on stage and hand me a microphone and I am in my element. Put me in a direct sales role and I clutch. Seems weird to me that these two things can exist in the same brain. The issue is exacerbated when given a choice in determining what to work on in that moment. As a GM of a business, I have a choice what to concentrate on in that hour. I can help define and support the product, or I can help sell the product. If I decide to help sell the product, I can work on marketing or I can work on sales.

At Ultimus, we inherited so many problems that it was easy to lose focus. By definition, turnarounds are like that. The CEO and I sat down early and divided up the company. I had North American Sales and Support, Global Marketing, and Global Product Development. Richard was going to concentrate on Finance, Global Sales (business units in Europe, Middle East, Central America and Asia), and our entire software development team (100+ skilled developers minus the CTO) in Pakistan. We had our hands full.

We had a new version of our software product (three+ years in development) coming out in a month, we had no training program in place, sales were stagnant or falling, competitors were taking market share, and every day we woke up wondering if we had a software team alive.

I am a builder—so I built, or rebuilt, the company. I let the sales people do their thing. I never called on a customer. I rarely went on a sales call. I built the business. Bad decision. And this was not the first time.

When I look back on every company I have ever run, I have just one regret—that I did not spend enough time on developing customers. Every company.

Customers rock.

Got your attention? You have a clear choice. Either develop your customer development skills or find someone who has them. Maybe he will serve as your co-founder. Maybe you can hire her. Either way, find this person and bring him or her into the fold.

■

Product development skills vary by product or, of course, by industry. Are you the builder of your product?

Have you spent time in the industry that makes you a credible builder? Think this through for a second. Do you have the skills necessary to build out the first phase of this product/service?

For most of you the answer is yes, but for different reasons than you may expect. It comes down to the definition of product. You will naturally define your product in its most perfect incarnation. You are thinking of the product three years from now when all the pieces are working perfectly and every customer will come to it like bees to a flower.

I, on the other hand, define it much differently. You can't afford to build that product right now. You will need something much simpler. You will need something you can put in front of a customer as soon as you can. You don't have the time or money to build something special right now. Your vision has outpaced the time allotted and your ability.

The types of people you need at this stage are the types of people who like to get things done. I earlier referenced the concept of personal momentum and how it can alter the psychology of fear. Product momentum has positive benefits as well.

For anything that has to be built (software, hardware, publishing, medical devices, pharmaceutical drugs) there is a product lifecycle. Managing the build-out of your first product is many times what differentiates the winners from the losers. Shoot too high and try to build too much, and either customers can't figure out what you are trying to do or you run out of money before you get a chance to build the Taj Mahal of your product.

In today's world, we have been conditioned to accept much less. Good product development people understand this and in fact use that understanding as a basis for their product's lifecycle. Experienced builders seem to balance the vision of the product three years from now and the team's ability to get something in customers' hands today. Your job is to surround yourself and your team with the types of builders who think that way.

No prima donnas allowed. They will kill you and your company.

Founders typically come from a product development background. You may be your own worst enemy. This is another reason why multiple-founder teams can fare better than a single founder. In a healthy founder-team environment, there should lots of room for pushback. Product debate should be front and center.

So some of you are thinking right now that this applies to everyone but you. Why? Because you are the next Steve Jobs, of course. Steve had the uncanny ability to see around corners. He did not need a customer feedback loop. But, he did have a great product development team who understood how to support his vision.

Don't get caught in the trap of thinking that you are Steve Jobs, Jeff Bezos, or Mark Zuckerberg. All of these solo founders really had great support co-founders or early partners. It's mostly a media fallacy. Stop reading and start thinking this through.

For the rest of us mere mortals, let's build a team of people who think the right way and augment each other's skills, experiences, and personalities, people we can trust and who can play a variety of roles when called upon.

The very nature and definition of The Startup Factory investment program is to take a small group (usually two or three; in fact the average is 2.42 founders per team) with a decent idea in an interesting product/market space and get them on a healthy startup trajectory.

The very structure of the founding team should be a consideration before launch time. I believe strongly that more founding teams should be created based on complimentary skill sets. We'll get to the psychology next. Too many "business" types and no programmer—you can't sell what you can't build. Get started this way and the two business guys will sit around dreaming of company systems that you will never get to implement.

Too many programmers and no one with sales/marketing experience—the product won't ever see the light of day. Who is going to represent the voice of the customer? By now I hope you understand how critical customer development is and how it needs to be addressed in the formative stages of the company.

First-time founders should outline the minimal team structure now and recruit the critical founding team members early so you can best leverage the energy and excitement before the dog days creep in.

There is much written around team dynamics and how they can drive early success. I will leave most of that to your next read. However, I do want to highlight a few thoughts tied directly to founding teams. Knowing that there will be really tough days ahead, how are you all going to deal with these issues when they inevitably show up? Yes, you can decide to figure them out by super-communicating in the crisis moment. Or, you can set up some rules of engagement going in that might serve you well when the beast arrives.

I met my current partner when I was canvassing the area in late 2009 while setting up the first incarnation of what is now The Startup Factory. I had moved the idea ahead over those first three to four months when I was encouraged by a few of the area's old guard to combine the idea with an existing entity that had operated two mentor sessions in 2008 and 2009. In the fall of 2010, we operated the first accelerator program in Research Triangle Park, or RTP, in North Carolina to much success. The program became a real catalyst for the community and, more important, for me; I knew exactly what I should be doing in my professional life.

Unfortunately the structure of that entity did not make sense and my team members (whom I had inherited, not chosen) were as dissatisfied with the relationship as I was.

So we blew it up.

Later in 2011, Dave reached out to me to ask if the concept for the investment program was still important to me, and if so, would I be interested in possibly working on it together. Sure. I knew this was my life's mission and was open to any discussion that could put this into play. But I was not willing to go through what I went through before.

So Dave and I dated. For three months we met about every week. We talked about the idea and how it would work and what we believed in, and what we each thought was important. Yes, we professionally dated so that we could eventually figure out if we were compatible and had complementary skills.

In the early days of our new business, Dave and I divided up the responsibilities necessary to get our it off the ground. He is strong in finance and legal. I despise the legal work. I am stronger in marketing and branding, and I had the experience of operating the first accelerator program. We decided that we each would take a turn leading a program and alternate back and forth. I would operate the first one, as I had lived it before. Dave would handle setting up the legal entities. I would get the website up and running, and I contributed the existing domain URL.

Each time we figured something out, we talked about it the following week to see if it still sat right. Each week we uncovered a new issue that needed to be discussed; we assigned responsibility for it and eventually completed the task.

During this period we learned how to work together and build the trust and respect required to get this new company off the ground. Dave taught me to discuss the tough issues as part of, and sometimes almost in spite of, the growing respect we had for each other.

I refer to Dave as my work wife. Interestingly enough, I was always criticized for not being able to work across an organization. I was great at managing up (supervisors) and even better managing down (direct reports) but working with peers was a hole in my skillset.

TSF has provided me the opportunity to get better at managing a partnership. You are never too old.

I talk a lot about fear. I'll say it again; it is the single biggest obstacle to success. If an individual's fear is a doozy, what about when the fear belonging to multiple team members invades the conference room at the same time? You don't think that you are the only one, right? So what are the chances that, of three founders, two of you are freaking out inside?

One way to deal with this is to get it out in the open early and assume that at any one time one of you will be having a freak-out day. Cross co-founder support is a pretty cool ingredient early in the company formation and is easy during the honeymoon period. Everyone should realize that doubt will creep into your psyche at some point. Why should someone have to wrestle with it alone? Why not provide a safe and supportive means for you or your co-founder to bring this out in the open?

This can be as simple as a statement to your team: "My head is in a bad place today and I need some help turning the evil around." Let's face it, our brains are evil some days, and the negative spiral that questions our abilities and vision can be a barrier to moving your idea forward. If one of your peers came to you with a coding issue, you would be happy to help them work through the solution. Why not the psychological blocks as well?

I have been deeply involved with at least 75 companies in my lifetime and have observed at least another 1,000 at some level of interaction. You start to see patterns emerge, and my eyes see team dynamic as one of the critical factors in startup success.

As a founder or co-founder of a team, you are responsible for setting the framework for how you are to execute the vision of the company. Regardless of whether you are a first-time team manager in a larger organization or the CEO of a new startup—you set the emotional tone for your team. When you commit to setting positive emotions your team invariably grabs that and makes that part of their emotional state. This is called *limbic resonance* and is a great tool for leaders. Limbic resonance is the theory that the capacity for sharing deep emotional states arises from the *limbic system* of the brain.

Emotions are contagious. Think of how much more you laugh with others when a funny story is told and everyone laughs together. The same goes for business emotions. When you create a daily environment filled with positive emotions every team member grabs hold and spins it back to you. You want to be part of that team!

Identifying and partnering with people who work well with you and your thoughts on how all of you will operate is a great starting point.

As your company gets started, there will naturally be euphoria. At this stage there are no limitations — only possibilities. I am smiling while I write this. This is the exciting part and I wish it could last forever.

Assuming that this will last forever, however, is a fool's belief. Difficult long days loom. But if you develop a sharing/safe team dynamic around all of the potential barriers at the outset, you may have reduced or eliminated future issues.

So, if I have you on board, your next question is how are you all going to create this kumbaya setting? If you are thinking like this, you have exaggerated the point of the story. I am not advocating sitting around singing or holding hands. I am pushing you personally and as a group to release the obvious psychological demons in a startup.

My current partner and I sit down two to three times per week at the start of the day and review what is on our mind. Most discussions are tactical, who is going to work on what. Sometimes they are more personal. On a few occasions I have shared that I have doubts about our investment portfolio's success. A few times I have wondered whether I was concentrating on the right tasks. These 10–20 minute discussions may sound squishy and not very CEO-like. That's OK if you want to think that, it's only our collective 50+ years of experience that drives us to have this open environment.

I don't care how you do it—just do it. Go off-site if you have to. Organize a dinner or head to the bar, just get to a place where you all feel comfortable exposing what's rumbling around your head no matter how trivial.

One of the things you need to be aware of, especially early in the journey, is "over-respect" for your peers' decisions. Maybe over-respect is too strong a term, but it means an unhealthy desire to make sure everyone is happy and no discord is allowed into the room.

An old boss of mine used to say, "Iron sharpens iron." Think of your company as a forged piece of steel that needs to become sharp and shiny. With a blank sheet of paper called your company and no customers or product, every decision is easy. The problem is that you have no reference point from which to push back on.

At this stage, you have a "group-think" mentality. It's dangerous for product decisions, as I outlined previously, and the early emphasis on customer development should balance that. Group-think can also signal a false positive about your team dynamic. You will all be looking at each other smiling, thinking that this company-building thing is pretty easy, as each of you is performing his or her role and there are no arguments, hiccups, or personality issues. Beware the false positive of team dynamics.

The ability for individuals to accept feedback is an interesting startup psychology. When recruiting co-founders or hiring your first employee(s), take into consideration how well they can operate in this type of environment.

In my fort-building story, Jimmy, Danny, Timmy, and I formed an initial team. Early on, Jimmy and I were acting as co-CEOs; Jimmy started the ball rolling by simply asking me to join him in building a new and better fort. The ask was made from a foundational understanding, as we had built forts before and we trusted each other. We had respect for each other. We were also 10 and we know that at 10, you don't carry much ego and adult baggage into the activity.

We then recruited two new members of the team, Danny and Timmy. Why?

The first reason was that we needed more bodies to make this happen. Jimmy and I had built many forts with just the two of us. These were simple forts that did not require anything more than the two of us could handle. But this fort was going to be different. It was going to be bigger and more "professional." It would have a roof and it would hold more than two people.

At this point, Jimmy and I discussed who we needed. I offered Danny with the reasoning that he had access to some materials we could use. We also knew Danny really well and understood what he brought to the table. The same goes for my brother Timmy. At that juncture in both of their lives, Danny and Timmy were more followers than leaders. It was understood that both of them were comfortable in their roles in building this new fort. The last test was asking them if they wanted to join the team.

The last question asked was, "Do you want to build a new fort—a fort that would be the best ever?" This served as the passion test and the analogies to creating a company are obvious. We wanted team members who engaged at the same high level as we did.

Earlier in this chapter, I mentioned my strong belief that entrepreneurship is a team sport, not a solo sport. Well, teams come in very different shapes and sizes and one of the notions we take seriously is the recruitment of advisor(s). In fact, one of the foundational elements of The Startup Factory manifesto is how you identify and recruit key advisors to your team.

Regardless of whether you are a first-time founder or if this is your third rodeo, advisors can help shape your vision. By definition, you have thought about a hundred different angles.

Advisors can help you eliminate, defer, and focus on the handful of critical issues you can afford to tackle at any one point in your journey. Good advisors have the ability to see through the noise and help you find the core of what you are trying to do.

Some of you are thinking that you will have to form an advisory committee like you read about in more mature companies. It does not have to operate like that. You can have multiple advisors who never see each other. You don't need to have a formal committee per se. Most startup CEOs recruit a cadre of one to three outside advisors whom they can lean on for sage advice. The great thing about good advisors is that they are not living every painful decision you and the team are faced with. Again, they can cut through the little things and nonessentials to help you focus on the larger issues.

So, how does one identify good advisors? If you are effectively socializing your idea, you are naturally going to run into potential advisors. Keep good notes, build a contact database, I don't care how you do it, but capture the skills and experiences of the people you meet. By remembering them when you meet them, you give yourself the ability to circle back to ask them to help.

There are formal and informal advisors. There are coffee meeting advisors and conference room advisors. There are compensated and noncompensated advisors. There are Year One and Year Three advisors. Advisors come in all shapes and sizes. There are no rules here and any way you want to work with an advisor is cool. What does this mean for you? It's simple and very similar to your task of finding a co-founder/partner: What do you need?

Let's go back to the fort for a brief second. In our story, we ran into an issue with building the roof. Remember that we were four 10-year-olds trying to figure out how to build a roof—something carpenters do every day but not so much for a couple of kids. We were way outside our league on this one. I am sure we could have figured it out eventually but to what quality? You can imagine a scenario where we would build something (a prototype, if you will), and then later tear it down or wait until it falls down. We would rebuild it, possibly improving it slightly with the same inevitable result. Eventually we would give up.

Instead we took a different approach.

In our search for wood, we ran across Mr. Conti and we socialized our idea with him. We did so with no ego, inhibition, or fear. Again, what did we have to lose—we were just a couple of 10-year-olds. Mr. Conti served as a perfect advisor for us. He asked us questions about what our goals were. He outlined a few of the big things we needed to focus on and walked us through how to get it done. He also brought some tools of his own to help us do it the right way the first time.

3
Gather the Assets
Closest to You

Every startup requires a minimum number of assets to get started. Regardless of whether you are starting a dry-cleaner or a software company, you need something that you can point to and say, "Do you want to buy that?" Certainly there is a huge difference between a dry-cleaner and the hard assets you need (machines to dry-clean—whatever they are) and the assets you need as a software company (programmers, marketers, etc.).

What you define as the minimum assets required to launch is your challenge. I have spoken at length about the emphasis on customer development over product development. At the very least, it needs to be a 50/50 allocation of resources. If I had my way, the split would be more like 70% for customer development and 30%

for product development over the first few months of the venture.

If you are to allocate only 30% of your resources to building out a product, that certainly de-emphasizes the value of the product and the natural result would be an inferior product. As a visionary with a clear picture of what the perfect product looks like, I would imagine that this would be quite disturbing.

Welcome to the new world of the **MVP**—the **minimal viable product**.

This concept is one of the critical underpinnings of the *Lean Startup* model as shared with us in Eric Ries's book (*Lean Startup*) and further popularized by Steve Blank (*Four Steps to the Epiphany*, *Startup Manual*) and Alexander Osterwalder (*Business Model Canvas*). This new-age triumvirate is the holy trinity of the software startup religion. Count me in as a disciple.

What is an MVP? If you buy the argument that your future customers need to be brought into the definition of the product earlier in the product development cycle (I hope you do), then it stands to reason that you should not build out the total product yet.

If you are not building out the whole product, then the argument would extend to say that you should build out the minimal amount of product that would solicit the most meaningful feedback. That is the concept of the MVP.

Determining the MVP unlocks your brain to identify the resources required now—not a year from now.

For the builder types reading this, I imagine that your head just exploded again. Put it back together and follow me for a little longer.

The tipping point for me was Google, circa 2004. Google released Gmail in an invitation-only beta release. No surprises there. What you may not remember is that it was opened to the public in "extended beta" in 2007. Three years later. The beta tag was officially removed in 2009 a full five years after its initial release. In my mind this was the first time a large technology brand signaled to its customers that their product had known flaws and missing features but they were going forward nonetheless.

Google set a new customer relationship tone for future web and app developers. Their message — it's OK if products are not perfect and in fact, we would like you to show us what you want and how you want to use our product.

How do customers do that?

The beauty of the Internet is the ability to track everything you do within the product. Word-only feedback is not sufficient and in fact can be misleading. Actions count for everything. To that end, it is imperative that you build into the product, on Day One, the hooks to track activity.

Ready to build out your MVP? Are you drinking the MVP Kool-Aid? Great, let's get started. First step — we need some stuff.

■

A good friend and an unbelievable entrepreneur shares this story as passed down to him by a mentor of his. It goes like this:

"What is the difference between 1 and 2?" The answer is obviously 1. The follow-up question is, "What is the difference between 0 and 1?"

The startup answer is not 1, it is infinity. For a company to grow metaphorically from 1 to 2, it has a known starting point and a known ending point. You are probably measuring the delta between revenue or customers, for example. For a company to go from 0 (an unknown point) to 1 (a known point) is hard. Really hard.

The difficulty lies in the unknown of the starting point, aka "0." The proverbial blank sheet of paper can be paralyzing. Once you get to your first milestone (let's say 100 customers) it is much easier to figure out your growth path to 500 customers. Peter Thiel addresses this in his book aptly titled *Zero to One*.

That is your challenge, to take a complete unknown with little or no data and get something started. The first thing you need to do is get something in front of your customers.

So, let's build a fort. What do we need?

For Jimmy and me sitting in Newtown Square, PA, the options for "stuff" were limited, to say the least. Or were they? The way kids would build a fort today would be to go get some money from Mom and Dad and then cajole one of them into going to Home Depot to pick up some wood. In fact, one of us might go online and order some preconfigured, build-your-own fort kit and either pick it up or have it shipped. For a few extra dollars, you might even hire someone to come put it together for you in your backyard. In the context of this story, I think I just vomited a little in my mouth. Neither Jimmy nor I would ever support this and I am really glad we did not have this option.

No, for us to build a fort we had to find our own materials and the materials had to be acquired without cash. There were no other options — like most startups. How does the saying go? *"Necessity is the mother of invention."* We needed materials for the fort so we went out and found some. In fact, we spent the first day doing nothing but scrounging for wood. If we broke down the entire fort-building experience, we allocated one-third of our time to gathering material for our prototype.

The metaphor in the story about acquiring the materials without cash is a strong one in today's startup world. My partner Dave and I have the opportunity to sit in front of hundreds of entrepreneurs a month. The meeting always starts with the budding entrepreneur sharing the vision for why his/her product will revolutionize a targeted industry. Too many times that is where the story ends.

My first question is always, "What have you accomplished so far?" Too many sit in our office fumbling for words that attempt to explain the barriers that are standing in their way. They then circle back around to pitching us the vision. Without any stuff or a prototype, it's the only thing they have. They then lament the position they are in.

It goes like this, "If only I had *fill-in-the-blank*, I could get this idea off the ground." The blanks include but are not limited to: a programmer, some data, a customer, cash for a salary. You get the idea. They want the equivalent of that online startup fort from the Home Depot. Being a CEO is about finding creative ways to gather resources with little to no cash—just like Jimmy and I did when building the fort.

Are you one of these wannabe startup founders? As they say in Texas, are you "all hat and no cattle?" Get up off your butt, get out of the office, and go get some stuff.

What kind of stuff do you need?

It always starts with people, in my mind. Why? Because I have limited skills. I am a generalist by definition, which means I know a little bit about a lot of things. Sound like a typical investor? Stop laughing. In order for me to get an idea off the ground I have to find people who are more skilled than me. That is where the socializing comes into play. While I am sharing my idea with people, I am also looking for potential partners who may be interested in joining me for this ride. If someone expresses interest and passion back to me, I then lock that away for future evaluation. Gathering people who can help is like gathering wood for a fort.

A few years back (around 2011), the tech scene in and around the RTP area of North Carolina was beginning to accelerate. As the pied piper and cheerleader of the area, I was privy to most of the newsworthy stories that were unfolding. And naturally as a cheerleader, I wanted to share that news with everyone else. At the same time, I was also frustrated that there was not a single source of basic background information on some of the more mature early-stage companies. So, I started thinking about a local news blog and started sharing that idea as I met with people in the area.

What if there was a central online place where you could go for information like who the founders were, or when they last raised money, or where their office was, or who their major customers were?

Not only would that serve as an excellent resource, it would create awareness for the region. That would be pretty cool, I said in my head, and then to about 20 people, over the spring of 2011. The feedback was positive and my excitement increased. Each conversation tightened the product. I was sharing product ideas and acquiring readers (customers) at the same time. Basic local company information about where the company was located and who the key executives were made it into the wish list. OK, enough of my vision is validated, now how do I get this off the ground?

Anthony and Katie are the ying and yang of Knurture—a new-age design and UI/UX firm that operates all over the country. Anthony had gone through an accelerator program in Washington, DC, a year or two back, and I had gotten to know him when I was validating the need for an accelerator program in RTP in 2010. I knew he had recently started his own design firm. I knew he was strongly opinionated and I knew he liked new ideas. So I pitched them on my idea for a crowd-sourced local tech blog and directory. It would be The Hacker News meets TechCrunch with crisp RTP walls.

They loved the idea. So we started pushing and pulling on the concept. At the same time, I met Megan who was a recent college journalism grad with two years of work experience. She was a glorified receptionist but had larger dreams. Megan and I formed an immediate connection as she was looking for something new to do, and I introduced her to a company I knew well that needed a good brain and a motivated employee. Of course I also socialized my idea of a community blog with Megan.

A few weeks later, I convened a meeting with Katie, Anthony, and Megan and a crisper vision of the idea evolved. As those discussions progressed, the skills, interests, and then roles evolved as well until we had a working team.

In effect, I had gathered the assets necessary to cobble something interesting together and get it out to the first readers. Anthony would design a website. Katie would keep Anthony on schedule and Megan was to recruit volunteer writers. I had access to what was going on and would play publisher and writer as well as cover the costs. *Triangle Tech Talk* was born.

No fear. No inhibition. If you clutch here, where else will you clutch? If you can't ask a few people to join your dream team how the heck are you going to raise money from investors or make the ask of a future customer? What was the worst that was going to happen; they would say No?

The interesting psychology here is that I had already paid it forward with both of these guys. For Knurture, I had made a few key introductions that resulted in their first customers. My intro had created a level of credibility in their pitch and later I served as a reference for them. For Megan, I had basically gotten her out of the receptionist job and into a high-growth company where she could take on marketing responsibilities — her ultimate goal.

They didn't owe me anything and I never went into it thinking that. But they did want to be part of something with a lofty goal that was bigger than each of us. That is what I was selling. That is what I am good at and it makes me a very effective startup CEO.

What other kinds of stuff might you need besides people? For most startups, there is a desire to know more about the target customers; how many are there, where do they hang out, how are they dealing with the issue you want to address today, etc. You get the idea. The good news is there is usually a research analyst that covers your target industry. The bad news is that they sell their research for hefty amounts of money.

Here is the best news of all—ignore that crap. It's a sham. Nobody gives a lick about his or her analyst research at this stage of the game. As an investor, I will categorically tell you that I will *never* make a seed or early-stage investment based on research from Gartner, Forrester, or IDC. It simply is not relevant. As an investor, I care about disrupting an industry—these organizations create product after the disruption has occurred. Do us all a favor and don't waste your time or money on paid research.

With that in mind, I do want to see some data, and customer data is what will turn me on. What kind of customer data do I want to see?

I want to know how many of your initial target customers are out there. I want to know where these target customers hang out (physically, virtually, digitally, behaviorally, etc.)

I want to see how many of those target customers you have engaged in some way. Have you talked to them? Have you pushed them to a landing page? Have you shown them sketches, wireframes, or back-of-the-envelope drawings? How many shared their email address with you? Have any given you their credit card information so they could pre-buy your product? These are all actionable customer signals that validate your idea.

I want to understand how you have acquired those target customers, or how you plan on acquiring them now AND later when you attempt to scale this company.

I want to know if they pay for a service similar to yours now. I want to know if there is any room to inflict some pricing pressure.

This is the type of data I want to see. This is the type of data that is an asset to the company. This is the type of data that can help form your MVP. Data is awesome and your first chance to separate your idea from the other startup ideas.

For the anal-retentive founders out there — stop freaking out. I know what you are thinking. This is not the time to overthink this data-gathering activity. We are not searching for a clinical trial for FDA approval. Five conversations are better than none. Twenty-five face-to-face interviews are better than five random conversations. Get out of the basement and gather some data.

What other kinds of stuff can we gather to support your MVP?

For those who have built a team of two or more people, you might think about finding some space where you all can work together. Does this sound frivolous in this Internet-connected day? Not so fast, Kemosabe.

Don't underestimate the power of the water cooler. I have run companies where we have all worked from our homes located all over the country, and I have run companies where everyone is sitting within 15 feet of each other. There is a large benefit — at this stage of the company—to have everyone within shouting distance of each other.

Remember *limbic resonance* that I discussed earlier? There is an obvious excitement in the first few months. Why not use that to your advantage? You all will feed off each other in ways you can't even imagine. That is one hallmark of the accelerator framework that The Startup Factory is based on. When we invest in our five to seven companies, we invest in all at the same time so that all of the companies and the founders/teammates are sitting in our space. Great collaborations occur that everyone finds extremely valuable. One plus one sometimes equals three. These are the benefits of shared space.

First, each individual founder and founding team sets their level of effort to the hardest-working founder or founding team in the space. Peer pressure. Some don't really know that they have another gear or that this gear is really important now. If you have spent the last 10 years at IBM working your 9–5 existence, you don't know that in Startupland, you are just getting started at 5 p.m.

Second, there is power in numbers. Sitting at the table next to you is someone who has skills and experiences that you don't have. Though they are working hard at their idea, there is an opportunity to share, help, and aid others in the room. We observe this all the time without any encouragement from us.

Third, by definition, a central gathering place for 10–20 startup founders is bound to be a place where interesting outsiders gather too. Investors, advisors, other startup founders, serial entrepreneurs— you get the idea. All of this makes for a very inspiring community stew. Why wouldn't you want to be part of something like that?

The positive team psychology is just one aspect. Peter Thiel writes about innovation as an incremental process where pieces of ideas are thrown together and assembled in ways that one person can't see but that a group can. Product development in the early stages should be a free-for-all. I want all my team members in the room for the organized discussions and the ad hoc, on-the-fly chats that will invariably spring up from nowhere. If your team members are holed up in their offices, you are missing an opportunity.

Do I have you convinced to go find some space? I knew you would come around. But here is the kicker—I don't want you to pay much or anything for this. If you are socializing the idea to the level you should, you will come across someone who has a crappy back office that is not being used. Ask them if they would let you use it for a few months. Offer to buy pizza for their employees once a month. Offer to help them for a few hours a week on their product/project. Give back something in return that is not cash. I love to barter for assets at this stage. Whatever you do, don't go sign a lease for more than 1 month. There are too many other options for you. Just ask around.

The same goes for furniture. Barter, baby! I have the same passion for office furniture that some women have for shoes; the more the merrier. I am always on the lookout for free, cheap furniture. Somewhere in your community there is a company going out of business. You should approach furniture the same way you should treat people and space — socialize your needs and see what falls from the universe. You will be amazed. Again, no fancy cherry-wood CEO desk needed at all. When starting Amazon, Jeff Bezos went to Home Depot and made his desk and the first number of employees' desks by screwing four legs to a wooden door.

For any of you thinking that this does not show well for future investors, customers, and employees, well then you are looking for the wrong investors, customers, and employees, in my opinion. The idea that you want to look the part before you can be the part is just old-school thinking. Startups need to be scrappy and that attitude starts from Day One.

When I relaunched The Startup Factory in January of 2012, I already had six Ikea desks and chairs that I had bought for $10 a desk and $5 a chair from a distressed gaming company. I then needed 20 simple tables and chairs, which I purchased from the previous owner of the space for $300 total. He didn't know what he was going to do with them. Everybody wins. They are just tables and chairs.

The final key asset for you to gather is capital. Old-fashioned cash. The gas that makes the car run. Gathering capital for your startup will be one of the hardest tasks you will ever perform as a founder or CEO. It is a skill that is acquired and not innate. All it takes is perseverance and a willingness to listen. I have raised capital and doled it out. Your heart beating fast? It should be. Relax, I will talk you through it.

Before we get into this, let me ask you one question — do you really need cash at this point? Don't answer so fast. I want you to really think about this. Knowing that this is very difficult and knowing that you only get good at it by getting your teeth kicked in a couple hundred times, do you really need cash right now to build your fort?

Jimmy and I were a couple of 10-year-olds in 1970. (Stop counting. Yes, it means I am getting old but I still have a full head of hair.) In 1970, there was no Home Depot. In 1970, families had one car and Dad took that car to work. In 1970, though my Dad worked at General Electric in downtown Philadelphia, we still occasionally used powdered milk (Mom mixed it with the real stuff so the combination was not too bad). It felt a lot like a startup, don't you think?

The point here is that finding $10 or $100 for materials for our fort was just not an option. Our fort-building team had to find assets that did not involve cash. We found it amazing what you can accomplish when cash is not an option. Creativity becomes your largest asset.

A cashless strategy makes you think broadly. Don't let pride or ego get in the way. Think like a 10-year-old who has little ego or misdirected pride.

One matter causes me the most grief as an early-stage investor. As mentioned before, my partner and I see 10–15 new startup founders a week. We operate at THE earliest stage of a company's development, so we are frequently connecting with first-time entrepreneurs. And the Internet is not their friend, because they have access to media coverage that frequently tells a highlight-reel story of "typical" success. If I didn't know better, I would easily assume that most people are able to raise whatever capital they need to get going. In fact, there are so many networking events today where any number of founders willingly share their fundraising anecdotes.

When you talk to them, you come away thinking, "Shoot, I am as smart if not smarter than they are!" Or you go the other way after meeting someone who has failed to raise money for his or her startup and think, "I am definitely smarter and better looking than they are. I can make this happen. This will be easy!"

This is a fool's errand. You are playing the wrong game. Rewire your brain now. Their success or failure has absolutely *no bearing* on your success or failure. It is the "compare game" like you played with your parents when you were 12. "Well, Suzy got a phone, why can't I?" you whined to your mom.

But you're not 12 and I am not your mom. I don't make investment decisions that way and you should not let that talk track enter your mind. Raising investment capital is hard and it should be. At its most basic level, it separates the wannabe's from the real entrepreneurs. It is Darwinistic. It is at some level survival of the fittest, or at least survival for the uber-serious and dedicated.

Later, I will go into more detail on how to raise the funds you may need to get started. But until then, let's make sure we consider all of the ways you can gather the necessary assets to get a crude version of your product/company off the ground *without capital*.

At this point, I have you convinced to find the stuff necessary to get this thing off the ground, which begs the next question: "Where do I find the stuff (people, data, research, customers, cash, etc.)?"

The answer lies in the socialization tour of course. Everything you need is available out in the world—you just have to identify it, find it and pitch it to be part of your startup. Sound simple enough? I can't reiterate this enough. You cannot get this off the ground while sitting in your basement in front of your computer.

One way to think about your socialization tour is that it never ends; it's merely a continual iteration of what you need at that point in time. Obviously your needs will change as this ramps up. Sometimes you will drive what you need and sometimes the feedback will shift your priorities to a new set of needs.

Let me give you an example:

Ricci has spent years in the banking industry, mostly in HR, and she gets frustrated at the slow process of onboarding new employees. There are approvals from the hiring manager, the head of HR, and the local branch manager. Then the new employees' basic information needs to be shared with the payroll department. Most of the communication is still through paper documents. This is just the tip of the iceberg.

So, Ricci sits up at night and dreams of a system that works through a secure Web browser and automatically routes the information to the right people at the right time without the use of interoffice mail. At any time, someone can go to the system and see where the process is and whose desk it is sitting on. At any time and from any location, Ricci wants to be able to check the status of that new hire when she is out recruiting.

Being a smart and diligent lady, Ricci asks her HR Director if they are aware of a system that would improve their onboarding processes. The Director says No. She also does a Web search for "new employee onboarding software." There are more than 300,000 results and when scanning through the top 10–15 she does not find anything about banking institutions. Great—no competition. Hooray!

But Ricci is into building a great fort and knows this is not enough. Her feedback loop has only one data point—her bank and her HR Director. She needs to go talk to a few more banks and a few more HR people to gather enough data so that her MVP is not wholly geared just toward her vision and her banks' needs but has a broader appeal amongst all banks.

Most ideas start with an issue we want solved for ourselves. There is nothing wrong with this as a starting point. It is, however, a big issue if you stop there.

By now you realize that the definition of your product will continue to change the more you talk to people. The result of this is that the assets and resources you need are also iterated along with the feedback. This can be a subtle or missed point of the tour for many first-timers. Stop. Think. What am I hearing that influences what I might need to pull this off over the next three months?

Three months? Really? But my vision is so much bigger. Basically, you have not earned the right to think beyond this time frame. Shoot too big and you never get enough data, traction, and momentum to get anyone interested.

Think in three-month chunks and ask yourself, "What do I need to get me to that three-month milestone?"

Once you have an idea of what you need, you now need to make a series of asks. This is where you separate the proverbial men and women from the boys and girls. Let me say this again, the role of the CEO is to gather the resources necessary to meet your goals. I outlined the different types of stuff you might need. I also pushed you to find cashless methods to procure that stuff. You don't get what you don't ask for. It's as simple as that. You will get a bunch of No's. Eventually you will get a Yes.

Make the ask.

A key element of making the ask is giving something back in return. Some will do it as a gesture of good will. Some may want to be compensated in return for their work. Stock options and cash or a mixture of both are typical. Sometimes you can get them to defer the cash until you raise some money later on when you have a product to show investors. Some want an experience that they can put on their resume. (This is a great one for recent college graduates wanting to break into a certain industry or role.) Part of your talk track is uncovering from them what they want and matching their needs with your needs.

In 2011 here in Durham, NC, I was just coming off the successful launch and operation of our first accelerator program here called LaunchBox Digital. Though it was clear that LaunchBox was not going to continue with the same people and the same name, I knew that somehow the accelerator concept was going to relaunch.

An integral part of operating a successful seed investment fund with a funky mentor program hanging off the side is placing yourself in the middle of all entrepreneurial action in the community. In that first year, I sat down and met one-on-one with more than 350 startup founders, investors, serial entrepreneurs, university professors, and anyone who even remotely played a role in the ecosystem.

One result of all of those meetings was a growing position as "someone who knows a lot of people." Malcolm Gladwell would refer to me as a connector and to this day, that one-on-one number would be closer to 2,500 people. As someone who knows a lot of people, I naturally get calls and emails.

"Hey Chris, I am looking for a software developer/marketer/sales person. Do you know anyone I should talk to?" As often as I get that call, I also get as many emails and calls that go like this, "Hey Chris, I am new to the area and am looking for a role as a developer/marketer/sales person. I understand you know a lot of people and companies and am wondering if you are familiar with any of the local companies' hiring needs?"

After a few months of this it occurred to me that there might be a business in here somewhere. In the spring of 2011, I created an event called *Tech Jobs Under the Big Top*. Everyone just refers to it today as the Big Top. The idea was simple. Can we create an event that does a better job of matching company needs with the desires of a set of job seekers?

So, I started socializing the idea to a few of my professional friends—especially to a few of the CEOs of the high-growth companies in the area—and out of those discussions developed a MVP version of the first event. The event MVP looked like this:

1 Make it fun for both parties. Job fairs suck for everyone. So I came up with an idea for an event around a circus theme; everyone loves a circus, right? We employ jugglers, acrobats, and clowns. We provide hot dogs, popcorn, peanuts, soda, water, and beer. Always beer.

2 Create an event based on equal footing for both the recruiter and the seeker. By leveling the playing field we represent what is reality in the tech field: seekers have all the leverage these days. So, companies stand on stage for three minutes and pitch the audience for the first half of the event. This subtle nuance creates a more level playing field.

3 Limit the number of companies so that they have a semi-exclusive ability to recruit. I select no more than 15 companies and the average has been more like 12–13 for any one event.

4 Create a diverse set of companies so that there is something for everyone. The companies range from 10–25 person startups to mature 500-employee companies. At any one event there are 100–150 open job positions.

5 The business model requires the companies to pay for the event and the job seekers attend for free.

What assets did we need to pull this off and test the concept? Here is what we came up with:

1 We needed an event space. I traded the cost of that for their right to be an exclusive sponsor. They received lots of brand placement in news coverage, online on the registration site, and at the event itself.

2 We needed a website. I traded the design and development of the website for another sponsor opportunity (bottom of website and at event) as well as personalized introductions to companies (lead generation) they had targeted for their own business needs. Thanks again, Knurture.

3 We needed food, acrobats, jugglers, beverages, and materials. We were able to pay for some with the fees paid by the companies and barter for some as they received awareness among the 300+ attendees.

I hated the idea of a traditional recruiting event. I wanted something special that was not your father's job fair. I also wanted to see if the concept worked, as it was pretty different from anything that had been done before. I had built up this long list of contacts in my day job (The Startup Factory), so I went to that list for help. I socialized the idea with those who would have a direct interest in the success of an event like this. I got them excited about the opportunity to be involved in something special. As a CEO or HR executive of a high-growth company, they were well aware of the challenges of recruiting new employees. The story was simple and went directly to their needs. Then I made the ask.

What is the ask? Simple. Joe and Chaz—would you like to have Bronto semi-exclusively participate in an event where you get to share your company's story with 300+ eager tech-oriented job seekers? The cost will be a fraction of what you spend for a recruiter or any employee introduction program.

Making the ask is hard for some people. It's a lot like sales and let's face it, some of us hate to sell. The thought process in our head says selling is convincing someone to do something they don't naturally want to do. This is crap and you need to exorcize this from your brain. Even used car salespeople don't think that way. When you show up at the car lot, you have already expressed a need for a car. The sales person is there to show you their availability and price and to create an opportunity for a match.

The same goes for your startup venture. When gathering the assets closest to you, you are simply trying to match your needs with their needs. Too many of us rationalize in our brains the final outcome before we even make the ask. "There is no reason they would ever want to *work with me*," you think.

In the Big Top story, I had the event-space people ask me if they could be part of the event before I even had a chance to ask them. Their strong need to be part of a unique event targeted at the demographic we would support compelled them to get onboard fast.

If you spend too much time gnashing in your mind whether people want to be involved with your new company, you have already failed the game. Your job is to gather the assets necessary to put your idea into play. Make the ask. We are all adults here and operate with free will. Make the ask.

Part of my premise is the idea that you have something to offer back. Here is where I need you to think more broadly and not just logically. Figuring out what you have to offer is difficult in many cases, but this is where you need to stretch. As a founder, you have the promise of something unbelievably special in the future. What if your idea explodes? In fact, not "if" but "when" is the thought you need to plant in everyone's head.

Every single one of us wants something we don't have today. It could be money. It could be glamor. It could be respect. It could be experience or access or just to be part of something different. It probably is a combination of these and a few more. Startups offer others the ability to achieve their personal goals. Your job is to figure out what drives people and attempt to match their goals with what your company can offer them. Believe me, it is an even trade and when it's not, everyone will know and a new set of expectations will be set. Let's worry about that later: remember we are thinking in three-month increments.

What you have to offer in return may appear to be a little squishy around the edges but I can tell you that there is real value in what you can trade back. You just have to listen and match.

■

If you did a postmortem on the failure of most startups, you would probably boil it down to a combination of two factors: too much friction and not enough time. When I am encouraging you to gather the assets closest to you, I am trying to position you to minimize friction.

Friction comes in many forms and all of them are deadly for a startup. Most of us think of friction as walls that need to be destroyed or navigated around. As natural problem solvers it makes sense that we identify issues and then deal with them. This thought process is too finite. I think of friction as more like quicksand to your company's progress. The visual is more like you and the team slowly and methodically step-by-step, inch-by-inch plodding through the muck. Your task is to reduce that friction so that everyone can get to the goals quicker with less effort. If you think of friction as walls, there are hundreds of mini-walls in the way. Yes, you can address every single one of those mini-walls but eventually you run out of energy. This is the friction of executing your idea. In the early days and weeks and months of your journey there are literally hundreds of mini-walls. I need you to identify three and needless to say, these should be whatever you consider the biggest three.

A better way to think about this is to operate above the quicksand and avoid many of those mini-walls altogether. Makes sense, Chris, but I am due back on earth now. What does this really mean for my company and me?

During the fort building, Jimmy and I identified a major goal of our next fort—a much-improved roof. This goal was so important that we made key decisions with that goal in mind. Think back to the decision to gather more wood so that it would be a better roof. Also remember the decision to stay a little longer with Mr. Conti in order to make a great roof rather than a quick roof. Identifying two to three of your major goals and then executing the smaller decisions within that framework quickly enables you to set consistent priorities, and more important, provides you permission to disregard other issues that creep into the day.

Typical friction elements include those around building product, getting customers on board through marketing and sales, hiring employees, finding space and furniture, and trying to raise investment capital. The slog of friction comes from spending needless time on needless tasks that are not important in this three-month sprint. You don't need to do everything yourself at this point.

■

When you start your venture with the idea to gather the assets closest to you, you invariably go to developing the product. Product development has changed a lot, even in just the last 15 years.

Today, there are any number of ways that we can "hack" something together. For software companies, the platforms available to build prototypes are endless. The issue that typically confronts startup software companies originates with an experienced tech founder or co-founder: tech founders want to code the perfect product. It is their wiring. They can't help themselves.

One of my favorite analogies is about the man who has a sore shoulder and when he meets with a surgeon is somewhat surprised when the surgeon wants to perform surgery to alleviate his problem. Surgeons cut. It's what they do. In this case, the man should consider meeting with a variety of alternative providers including a chiropractor, a physical therapist, and the surgeon.

For a software company, developing every line of code alone or internally instead of utilizing existing open-source modules or platforms is just plain arrogant. Remember, your goal is to get something out to market with as little friction as possible to validate that a customer actually wants to use your product.

In every application there is the critical "secret sauce" and there are the parts that just don't matter.

Identify those critical secret sauce pieces and hack the rest from another source. Developing those parts in-house with your limited resources wastes time and creates additional points of friction. Socialize with others specifically what you are looking for and you will find ample avenues for integrating those borrowed parts into your MVP.

But beware. You will get pushback from the tech lead in your company. Is that you? You must find a way to get balance in that discussion either inside your head or with someone else. (This is a great place for a product-oriented advisor.) If you are the nontech part of the team, you must ask the tough questions and drive to find the best answers. Question your tech partner without fear or inhibition.

"Is there a shorter way to build this section out?" You ask your tech team.

Failure to do so typically results in one of two outcomes: (1) the perfect 100% internally developed product never gets completed as funds, energy, and people are exhausted; or (2) the perfect product (in the team's eye) is completed but totally misses the market and nobody cares.

Your job: develop a great team where these types of discussions can take place with little ego or angst. Then drive those discussions to identify the parts that are not critical and what parts are critical. At this stage, find a way to gather the critical parts as quickly and cheaply as possible. Don't worry about the rest now.

■

Identifying and acquiring initial customers is the hardest element of a startup, in my opinion. As I place more and more pressure on our investments from The

Startup Factory to develop these muscles, I find myself looking back on the companies I have led with regret. There is not a day that goes by when I don't think to myself, "Chris—you needed to spend more time on acquiring customers."

Regardless of whether you are going to do direct sales or use online marketing, the pressure is on to get the customer feedback loop started. Herein lies an opportunity for massive friction. Your job is to find ways to gather the customer assets closest to you and reduce or eliminate this friction.

For many web software or mobile application companies, there is no secret sauce in the code. What I mean by that is that there is no special algorithm or technical breakthrough that defines the product or company.

For example, I would say that Etsy had no real IP in their code when they launched. In this case, the vision was more about creating a marketplace for a targeted demographic that had a need that was not being met. Twitter is a great example of this. In its early formation, there was nothing inherently special about the underlying code. Their challenge was to identify, market to, and acquire a critical number of users to their platform. In fact their secret sauce was more about creating a viral effect for acquisition than it was about writing perfect product code.

So, is customer acquisition your secret sauce? Then you must be integrally involved in the customer funnel of your business.

For you and your company, let's start by reexamining that three-month window. What are your realistic customer acquisition goals for that time period?

For a business application, we might be thinking 10 customers. For a consumer or social product, we might be thinking of something more like 1,000 users/customers. The customer acquisition strategy will clearly be different for those two scenarios.

To reduce friction, you need to map your acquisition strategy to those three-month goals. Don't get hung up on the strategy of the three-year vision. That is a deadly trap. You don't have the time or money to execute those tactics right now. Feel secure in the opportunity to create customer momentum with a realistic number of initial customers.

So, what tactic or small set of tactics do you need and what kind of help do you need to execute those tactics? Are you going the direct sales route to acquire 10 beta customers?

No need to hire a sales person — get out there and sell this yourself. Make a list of the potential customer companies (keep them local if you can so that you can service them face-to-face). Use LinkedIn to identify the target person in each of those companies. Craft a way to get a warm email introduction to those targets through a mutual friend.

Need 1,000 or more customers? Direct sales won't work and you can't afford enough sales people to sell directly to them anyway. You will need to test a series of online marketing campaigns. Successful marketing is a recipe in which the ingredients are well known but the amount and mixture of those ingredients varies for every product and every target audience. This is why you have to own this recipe early. An outsourced marketing service can execute the tactics but they will never fully understand the product or customer like you do.

One of the best-known terms used today to uncover the recipe for marketing is *growth-hacking*. A person involved with this activity is a growth-hacker.

It's a phrase that I embrace, and credit is due to Sean Ellis for coining the term in 2010. The genesis of the term is a mash up of *growth*, which should be obvious and refers to the goal of growing your user base, and *hacking,* which comes from the programmer culture and gets to the notion of utilizing a combination of curiosity, cleverness, and skill to execute a task quickly and at a low cost. Sounds like our kind of activity for a startup, right?

When you are thinking about gathering the marketing assets closest to you, you will find a plethora of avenues to explore. There are websites, tools, blogs, and conferences that will fill your head with best practices. Depending on where you live, there are also marketing operators who are experienced in applying online marketing strategies to grow their user base. I would look to similar companies in your area who have achieved some level of success growing their own user base using marketing techniques. Remember: socialize what you need with as many different people as possible. Go talk to the experts on the front end of their company. I promise you they will share their war stories with you. The bottom line is, explore a mix of these avenues and then learn how to apply them to your recipe.

If you are one of those companies whose secret sauce is identifying and acquiring customers, then you need to own customer acquisition from the start.

Too many companies miss this dynamic. The founder somehow gets caught up in the role of playing CEO, and that role has them playing traffic cop to all of the resources they have gathered. If you are removing yourself from all of the key components of the business, I fear you will never find your secret sauce.

Will you need to hire experts (or even just a few live bodies) to get some stuff done? This is another area where playing CEO logic can get in the way and actually create friction. By definition, you don't know what you are yet, right? So how do you know what you need to hire? So many waste time and money hiring experts for a company years out—the three-year vision of what the company will be. Remember, three months is our target. What do you need to accomplish the goals for that time period? In most cases, the need is temporary, so act on that fact. Do you need someone to design your home page? Don't hire a full-time designer; you can't afford this person and frankly your product and company don't need it. You need a quick design burst that gives you a little credibility with potential customers. You should be thinking, "Where can I hack a designer?"

Is there a local art institute you can talk to? Is there a meetup in your town for local designers to talk shop?

Go show up there and sell what you need. No doubt you have come across a few small design shops. Talk to them about your startup vision and where you are and convince them to do something for little to no upfront cash. They once were where you are. The promise for them is that when you take off and have some funding, they will get the bigger work. Match what they want with what you need.

■

The one asset that we all think about is cash, cash for ourselves (how do we live) and cash for various aspects of the business. I mentioned before how too many of us make this a criterion for actually launching the business, and that's a shame. Deep down, I believe that if you need someone else's cash to launch your business then you are not truly an entrepreneur. This includes your family as well as outside investors.

Raising investment dollars on an idea today is foolish. The only people able to make this happen are previously successful founders. For the rest of us, we must raise money based on data and traction.

This chapter has been about finding cashless ways to gather the assets necessary to create data and traction, to "build the fort." In some cases though, you may need a minimal amount of cash to procure certain must-haves. The first person you should look to for cash is you.

I don't care if you are 20 or 50: there are ways to

find a few thousand dollars. I am not advocating selling your blood, semen, or eggs here. (Eggs get the most money, guys, FYI.) I am talking about operating your life at its bare minimum. Just graduated from college? Then sacrifice and ask to move in with your parents or couch surf at your buddy's apartment. Are you a little older and have you been working for the last eight years in a professional job? Then cut back on your lifestyle for the preceding six months and save some money. Your sacrifice has to equal your passion for making this happen.

Raising money is very difficult. It is a grind. There are many barriers standing in the way. Think walls AND quicksand combined. Eliminate or minimize the amount of dollars needed to launch and get through the next three months. Putting fundraising in front of the decision to leap is insane.

As an investor, I hate the conversation with a soon-to-be entrepreneur where they share that if only they could raise X thousand dollars, they would quit their job and get started. Then they drive away in their Mercedes. What sacrifice have they made to make this happen? It feels like they want me to fund their risk.

After you exploit everything you can do, then, and only then, should you turn to other investors.

■

Closely related to friction is time and, as the saying goes, time is not your friend. Good startup ideas die because the team could not execute fast enough. Fast enough for what? Time constrains everything in a startup, including time to the first customer, time to hire the right people, time to get enough product traction to be meaningful in a customer's eye. Everything takes longer than expected. Dreamers fail because they could not execute fast enough.

So how do you optimize for time? Winners optimize time by concentrating on the parts of the business that are critical at this immediate moment. Winners win because they figured out the minimal set of tasks required to get to the next milestone. Winners don't run out of time.

I see startup success as a series of three-month sprints that all add up to a marathon. This time frame is somewhat arbitrary, so if you need to come up with something more appropriate for you and your company, go for it. However, if you set a milestone much longer than six months, I am sure you are missing the point of gathering the assets closest to you. Your asset-gathering tasks must be in sync with what the team can accomplish without losing energy, traction, or momentum.

The premise of channeling your inner 10-year-old has many ramifications, and the appropriate use of time is a critical factor. As a typical 10-year-old, you have a psychological/biological limit to your ability to focus on any one activity. In my example of building the fort, Jimmy and I allocated no more than a few hours a day for gathering the material necessary for starting the fort.

Why? As the leaders of this fort-building startup, we

knew that we had to get to the fun sooner rather than later. We knew we would lose Danny at some point, as he lost interest quicker than anyone else. And Timmy had other interests besides helping us build a fort. We could count on them for pieces of this fort building for discrete periods of time, but to rely on them to help us for a week or two would be just dumb.

So, we gathered the assets closest to us to optimize time and reduce friction.

Let's play out a couple other optional scenarios as set in 1970. We could have asked our mothers to drive us to another neighborhood to find material. This might have worked if she had a car (Dad had it at work). We could have waited until the weekend to ask our dads to help build the fort with us. (Jimmy's dad had passed away in a military accident and my dad could not nail two pieces of wood together.) We could have scrounged for materials as one group instead of splitting up into two. (This would have effectively cut our productivity in half; the material gathering might have taken two to three times longer and we might have lost interest after a time.) We could have pooled any allowances or savings together in order to purchase some material. (I know Timmy would have never agreed to that, as he was saving for some swim flippers.)

Within a day of verbalizing the idea to build a fort, we were building a fort. We allocated a few hours to inventorying the materials available to us. (This still makes me laugh a little.) We gathered those materials very quickly and were digging soon thereafter.

It is clear that fort building has a limited time allotment and a minimal friction allowance. Your startup is no different. In fact, your co-founders and peers are probably more like Danny and Timmy than any of us ever realize. When you think back to your fort-building experiences, think about how you inherently optimized for both friction and time. It seemed to come naturally to all of us then — let's make sure we channel that today.

The last thought on gathering the assets closest to you is the idea of "good enough." "Perfection is the enemy of the good" is a quote from Voltaire that my partner Dave uses frequently, and it applies in spades to startups. If you or your partners are perfection freaks, you are in big trouble. There is absolutely no room in a startup for this type of thinking. I bet I got your attention now!

There is a certain amount of arrogance in thinking that you 100% understand how your product should operate. Product iteration is at the core of every company, including Apple. The iPhone is not a breakthrough from a cellular phone perspective. A cellular phone with a touchscreen interface is an innovation but I would argue it is an iteration on an old design. Perfectly designed product that no one cares about is a waste of your time and potentially your investor's money.

Let's be honest, we all know someone who plays the "quality is the only attribute worth measuring" argument at every meeting. *There is no room for that person in a startup.* So how do you guard against letting team members manage to some perfection standard?

First, you need to identify that person early in your socialization/recruitment journey. What does a person like that sound like? Here are a few red flags:

1 They talk in absolutes. This product is either perfect or is completely flawed. One way to see if you are compatible is to sit together and evaluate a few products that are not in your field of interest. By selecting "safe" products, you will not fall into the trap of describing every competitive product as weak.

2 They focus on minute details. Talk about the last few projects or products that each of you worked on and share items that you are proud of and a few that were frustrating. Dig in deep on the features you wished could have made it in and listen to the tone of those details.

3 They lack patience and are workaholics. These types stop at nothing to achieve their lofty goals. Work-life balance gets thrown out the window in a nanosecond when things don't go their way.

The best way to flush out this type of teammate is to work on something together. It is one reason why I suggest working in the same room with your co-founder.

The best way to guard against perfectionism creeping in is to let your customers drive more of your decisions. I hope I have made an effective argument for getting something in front of your customers sooner rather than later. Set up correctly, your customers and the customer feedback loop will showcase where your product needs to be at any one point in time.

I have hacked more initial product than I can even remember. Soon after coming out of graduate school in 1984, I went to work for the US State Department in the Bureau of Intelligence and Research. The bureau had an Office of the Geographer and the mission of that office was twofold. One mission was to research a variety of current global issues from a geographic perspective. But the mission I was asked to lead involved the four cartographers in our office. They were tasked with creating custom one-off maps to support the office, bureau, and department.

The majority of maps we created were page size or smaller, as they were to augment the written words of a research piece. The maps were critical to the piece but were very simple in their design and output. The state of custom cartography for simple page size or smaller maps circa 1984 involved the use of pen and ink. (Did your head just blow up, too?) Typical turnaround times were in the 6–12 hours-per-map range, which meant that only the research documents with longer lead times could have integrated maps: any burning global issue that had exploded that day or the night before could not get a map unless we worked overnight. (Think Chernobyl or the bombing of Libya.)

Of course I had no idea how to use pen and ink and

was not satisfied with a 6–12 hour turnaround time. In addition I was an aggressive personality who wanted to improve our credibility and standing within the bureau by serving the sexier, more relevant issues of the day.

So, how did I hack something together with no budget and little computer resources? GIS (Geographic Information System) platforms were too expensive and very difficult to operate for a group of traditional cartographers. I needed something that resembled their current skills and process but offered shortcuts to the more mundane and repetitive cartographic tasks, like drawing a shoreline or country boundary.

A number of crude geographic databases were available to us, as most of them had been created by a number of government agencies. I reached out to a few and procured free copies. I then turned to an existing drawing platform used exclusively by architects at the time called AutoCAD. The beauty of AutoCAD circa 1984 is that it gave users the ability to import various layers of line work—in my case shorelines, rivers, and city, state, and country boundaries.

I reached out to a colleague back in the lab I'd worked in at graduate school who was very fluent and skilled in geo-data manipulation, and I paid him to write an interface that brought the geographic data into AutoCAD. After that, the only thing left to do was teach the cartographers how to use AutoCAD to complete their map.

Within six months, we cut the average map production time from 6–12 hours to less than 4 hours.

By utilizing off-the-shelf software, a number of free datasets and a custom software tool to bridge the data and software, we created a new map production platform that put the office and our services front and center. We were now relevant.

The map platform was not fancy by any standard. I did not care what it looked like and I did not care how others (the CIA) viewed our platform from the outside. All I wanted to do was serve our customer base faster. Those first few maps were not pretty but they were produced quickly. The cartographers got to know the tools better and had opportunities to be trained by experts. In addition, we found more datasets that were later integrated into the production platform, which broadened the richness of each map and further cut production time.

The map production "fort" was cobbled together from a collection of disparate pieces that were easily gathered and were within arm's reach. If I had been driven by perfection, I easily could have spent another year budgeting for a more expensive system and then spent another six months training the cartographers. That was not an option for the office or me.

In essence, our system managed time, which ultimately was how the rest of the bureau judged us. Our system was good enough and in that state we were able to extend the services that addressed the real needs of our customer.

4
Create a Short-Term Collective Purpose

The fourth element of building the fort is centered on the scope and pace of company progress. As a crawl-walk-run advisor, I strongly push founders to define a short-term collective purpose. At different times so far, I have discussed the trap of building toward a grand vision out-of-the-gate.

On one hand, each of us makes the decision to leap with the promise of what could be. That vision has all of the elements of the business operating perfectly together. We have marketing, acquiring targeted customers, and those customers using a number of the features that are built into our product. In our vision, we service those customers with a hands-on support team that perfectly inspires our customers to love our product/service. Our software development team is working each new feature as we extend the platform into relatable industries. As a result of this well-oiled machine, we spend more of our time managing an executive team that has responsibility for each one of those areas. Our company is near perfect, we dream. I did it!

But, how do you get there? This vision is three to five years out at best. And, that is IF you get there. Your vision, as perfect as it appears, is unattainable at this startup moment. Assuming that you will succeed is a healthy part of your personal psychology. But your vision is too big, and operating on a plan three years out is flawed. You cannot execute on this version of your company. Let's dig in a little deeper.

At the very core of an entrepreneur is someone who sees something others cannot see yet. The largesse of the vision by definition has little specificity. That is what makes it easy and that is what makes it impossible to execute today.

You have to earn your right to get to that grand vision. You get there by starting the journey with small steps. Those steps are the three-month goals we discussed previously. There are many examples of executing small steps to build big companies if you dig deep enough to see them.

Let's peel back the rise of Facebook:

You've seen the movie so this should be clear. Mark wanted to get laid. Mark had an engineer's mentality so getting laid was not likely. Mark and his friends needed a way to engage online with girls so that they could increase their chances for connecting. What Mark and his co-founders did not set out to create was the world's largest social media platform where two billion plus users share pictures, life moments, and history. No, in February of 2004, *The Facebook* was built for Harvard students to connect to other Harvard students.

Though I am sure that Mark and team at times dreamed of a platform that addressed the needs outside Harvard, I would guess that dream extended only to other colleges. Soon after launching The Facebook to Harvard students, the team added other local Boston colleges, then other Ivy League schools, and then Stanford University.

The important lesson here is that great companies execute on smaller, attainable mini-visions, which then enables them to extend their product into newer areas. For Facebook that eventually meant noncollege students. Only in September of 2006 — more than two years later — did the site become the site we know today.

Great companies evolve from smaller companies. Smaller companies have smaller goals. Smaller companies have simpler plans. For Facebook that meant nailing (all puns intended) the Harvard experience and only then expanding past their local users.

The CEO psychology here is wicked. All we have to do is look around us and engage our startup radar and we will pick up lots of information that skews our perception on how it should be done. It takes an awfully self-aware startup CEO to navigate these waters effectively.

Sure you get buy-in from co-founders, employees, partners, customers, and investors by selling an exciting big vision for what could be. Let's face it—it is exciting to tell the big story and honestly, it makes us feel important. It also feels smart, as in "I know something you don't."

The arrogance of this thought could kill your company. There are countless startup articles, books, and podcasts that remind you that it is the execution of the idea, not the idea itself, that wins the day. So trying to play the "I am smarter than you" card is pointless.

But the media tells a much different story. We see Jeff Bezos featured in *Time* magazine or Travis Kalanick of Uber at TechCrunch Disrupt and say to ourselves, "I want to be a CEO just like them." These and others with equal success sit on a stage sharing insights and witty quips about where their company is going and how they will conquer the world.

Startup founders—this is not reality. This behavior had absolutely nothing to do with their early startup success. It is a result of their success, not an ingredient of their initial success recipe. Spending time thinking of ways to appear smart and witty in front of the press will not get your startup off the ground.

So Chris, what good is a big vision if I can't think about it and make it part of my story? My advice: treat the vision as a special tool to be used in special situations only. Bring it out only when needed and then put it away just as quickly. Don't define yourself or your company by the vision alone.

The fourth element of building the fort is about defining a short-term collective purpose. Again, the time period is up to you. But, in general, six months is too long and one month is too short. The time horizon that works best for you and your company should map to the expectations that others have shared via your socialization tour.

For example, if you determine that you need to raise investment capital within the first year and the feedback from investors is that you need 15 paying customers before they would consider an investment, then you need to plan for how to get to 15 paying customers. Sounds simple but many blindly ignore the feedback and trudge along building a better product with no customers. If that is you, don't bitch to me six months later that investors just don't see the magic in your beautiful product. You either did not solicit the data necessary or you ignored the data completely.

When our investments at The Startup Factory are preparing their final pitch at our Showcase event, the pitch feedback invariably comes around to "how much vision versus how much traction." The thinking from the presenter is always "Let's sell the vision." The pushback from us is sell the traction and dribble in the vision at the end. The ratio we advise is close to 95% traction and 5% vision.

We talked about the MVP (Minimum Viable Product) and how it creates a stress point for the company. The idea is that the feedback is valuable regardless of whether it is good or bad. Bad feedback reveals flaws in your thinking. Uncovering that feedback sooner enables you to make adjustments that save you time and money.

Sounds good. But how do we define what an MVP is? We can argue all night long about what the minimum is and what the product should be. So I guess the key word in this exercise is viable. Merriam-Webster defines viable as "capable of being done or used" and "having a reasonable chance of succeeding." Talk about a letdown. What the heck does that really mean? If this was a debate on glass half-full or glass half-empty, I think empty just won by a landslide.

We'll get back to viable and minimum in a few because it turns out that the keyword in MVP is product. Why? Because your first thought is that you have to put some version of your product in front of someone in order to get a level of valuable feedback.

Wrong!

There are a number of ways we can get interesting feedback data before we write a line of code. Eric Ries's <u>Lean Startup</u> outlines a number of options. Here are a few more to bend your brain a little.

Today, email represents the most common way we engage with other people. Or machines. Or companies. Don't believe what you read about a spam epidemic. Like it or not, we click on email from people we don't know all the time. Why? Because more times than not we get something valuable in return. So we are willing to take a chance unless the spam is overwhelmingly obvious.

ReverbNation is one of the nation's leading online

toolsets for musicians and bands. Their comprehensive set of services enables more than three million bands to market themselves to their hopefully growing fan base. Musicians use ReverbNation to upload their music onto their own website. They use ReverbNation to push email to their bands' subscriber list, and ReverbNation offers tools for bands to advertise themselves on online paid platforms like Facebook and Google AdWords. The tools that ReverbNation offers are solidly tested and provide incredible value to their customers, their musician customers.

But Jed and Mike wondered if there were others besides musicians who operated similarly and wondered if those professionals could use some of these marketing tools as well. When Jed and Mike started ReverbNation 10 years ago, the startup methodologies were quite different but today, with all the customer development thinking, they decided to apply this to a new market.

They first made a list of more than 50 similar industry operators including authors, poets, speakers, realtors, and many more. They then selected just one, realtors, as a test. They had a couple of questions. The first thing they wanted to know was what tools realtors might want. They also wanted to know how realtors marketed themselves today.

So Jed decided to use email as the tool to answer these questions. The first thing he did was build an email list of realtors across the country. The list included their name, their firm, their location, and their email address.

The second task was to research and outline a series of interesting factoids that realtors would find of interest.

With a one-million-strong realtor email list, a bucket of interesting realtor facts, and a hint of what types of tools a realtor may want, ReverbNation started emailing the list.

Today, a new business—Adwerx—has launched and has exceeded everyone's wildest expectations. The total time to market and the revenue ramp up for these guys is a phenomenal startup story. More so, it is a phenomenal customer development story where the interests and needs of a targeted customer set were uncovered before a product was put into play. Well done, guys! They executed a lean startup business perfectly.

My favorite brain tease when listening to an entrepreneur outline her vision for her company is the question, "How can we uncover customer sentiment without building the product?" For almost every Web or mobile app, the answer is the landing page. Landing pages are typically one-page websites that have a simple message and a distinct call-to-action.

A landing page is simple to craft and in fact there are literally hundreds of companies and tools available to create one in minutes. With that in mind, what does a landing page do? The purpose of a landing page when used early in a company's formation is to solicit actionable feedback from a customer base. Hence the call-to-action element I outlined above.

For example, I have an idea for selling Philadelphia Flyers memorabilia (my favorite team and obsession).

Before I spend weeks or months developing or hiring an expert to develop a website with pictures, descriptions, and an ecommerce back-end complete with the credit card transaction capability, I would like to know how many interested customers are out there. Maybe there are five of us, including my mother (the biggest Flyers fan of all). That would be bad, with such a small customers base to sell to.

The customer development thinking here is let's put up a one-page website (actually a series of alternate landing pages for one website address) with a request to share your email if you want to be put on a weekly newsletter highlighting that week's featured memorabilia. For someone to share their email means they are pretty serious. Now let's spend some advertising dollars to drive traffic to the website (complete with the alternate A-B-C versions of the designed page) and gauge interest by measuring click-through's to the site, the amount of traffic, and the number of email subscriptions. In this scenario, the landing page test would reveal a number of key insights including:

- What type of advertising drives the most traffic?
- How much does that advertising cost?
- How many potential customers are out there?
- What is the cost of acquiring an email address?

From here I can make some pretty compelling assumptions about my future business prospects before I spend a minute or a dime on developing the full website, aka my product.

With regard to a short-term collective purpose, this landing page scenario and its resulting data fit perfectly into a three-month set of goals. During this time period, I have unlocked what it takes to acquire a customer and have a good idea of which messaging seems to resonate the best.

When getting started, don't fall into the trap of thinking that your MVP has to actually be about your product. There are many ways you can gather information before starting to build product. In fact, this is clearly a task you can execute without expert developers. There is nothing to hold you back from running a series of low-tech tests today unless you are afraid of the answer.

For some, answers, insights, and data might reveal that their idea is bad or at the very least not ready for prime time. Is that you? Are you going to be one of those entrepreneurs who enjoys playing the role of entrepreneur more than the task of building a company? If you are afraid of determining the validity of your idea then you are not a good entrepreneur.

A prototype is a starting point for your product. It is the first glimpse of how your product delivers just a hint of value. In many ways, the prototype and MVP are synonymous. Certainly the goals are the same for both. The prototype is not for sale. The prototype is not public. The prototype is a working example of what could be. It could be your vision or most likely a subset of your vision. The prototype or MVP is your first opportunity to see how things might work. For many who have to visualize something to understand it, the prototype is the object you can point to and say, look at this! A product idea locked in your head has no value to anyone else. The prototype is your limited coming-out party.

The conundrum is between having pride in something closer to fully baked and that shows well visually versus the sheer fear of putting a raw prototype that is pretty rough in front of someone you respect. Why would anyone choose the latter? You can't get feedback if you don't show something to someone.

Earlier we discussed momentum and the important role it plays in the first year of your startup. It is your job to create meaningful, realistic, and achievable milestones for the company. The three-month horizon should allow you to craft a number of interim success points that support your mission. With those clearly defined points outlined, it is now up to you to execute to those points.

For the Newtown Square fort-builders in 1970, our short-term collective purpose was simple. No Taj Mahal dreams here. We were not trying to build a house or even a fort by today's Home Depot–inspired standard (the kit with windows and doors.) No, we just wanted to build a slightly upgraded fort that was a little bigger than previous forts and where we had a roof that did not leak rainwater.

Simple. Achievable. And well within our reach for the patience of four 10-year-olds.

The beauty of the fort analogy is that as a group of 10-year-olds, we didn't know better. There was no media model glamorizing the Taj Mahal of forts. We were defined only by our own definition of what a fort could be. (No Tree Fort reality TV show for us. By the way, there really is a show today, and it is very cool, called Tree Fort Masters on Animal Planet.) At its core, Jimmy and I knew that we had about three days max to keep the team in place. So we outlined our three-day plan and scaled our tasks to meet that simple goal.

If we reached at all, it was for a better roof. And that is where our advisor, Mr. Conti, came in. You see, Mr. Conti was the bridge from what we could achieve to what we did achieve; he stretched our reach to fulfill our dream. Mr. Conti taught us how to create the roof frame while at the same time keeping us focused within the rough framework of our dream. How easy would it have been for him to extend our dream to something closer to his vision? At that point, the fort would have doubled in build time and we would have lost Danny and Timmy, been short of material, and probably lost interest.

Mr. Conti's advice fit the scope of our short-term collective purpose. (Great job, Mr. Conti. I miss you, Mrs. Conti, your pool, and your horseshoe pit. A lot.)

5
Build the Fort

Every journey starts with the first step. It's a little cliché but how appropriate is it here in this entrepreneurial context? Over the course of this book I have likened the weeks and months leading up to your startup leap to building a fort as that 10-year-old kid. Think back, close your eyes, and try to feel like the 10-year-old version of you.

Was there fear?

Was there doubt?

Was there a moment when you thought this was a life or death decision?

There was only that one thought—**I can do this**.

At many times during my career I was faced with the decision to jump into the unknown of my next idea. Sometimes my feet did not move. But sometimes I jumped. The more I jump, the easier each jump gets.

Starting a company is easiest when you have the right mindset. The decision to throw whatever existing job or role away is scary and as adults we are really good at manufacturing fear. My Dad once said that if you applied only logic to having a child, then you would never ever make the decision to do so. Having a kid defies logic. No amount of pros can offset the logical cons in the pro versus con list. Doing a startup is like having your first child. The decision is more of a leap of faith than a logical step.

An obvious part of our fear is the fear of what we don't know. It's all those hundreds of decisions way out in the future that we cannot control or manage, yet alone see, from our cozy spot today. As a first-time entrepreneur, the journey is as unknown as it was for Christopher Columbus on his first trip west from Spain.

The four steps I have already outlined to building a fort alleviate the scary parts of the startup leap by sketching out a few simple steps to get your idea off the ground and put your company into the game. My hope for you is that you channel that 10-year-old girl or boy inside. That person looked at the world in simple terms with achievable goals and no fear of failure.

The first step: **socialize the idea without fear or inhibition.** Laugh at what you don't know. Spit in the face of the demons who shout, "You are not ready." There is an insane amount of personal power in the collective feedback of many. Go find that feedback and bring it back with you.

While on that journey, inventory then **partner with skilled and trustworthy people.** I don't mean in

a Hannibal Lector–*Silence of the Lambs* creepy way.
Socialize your company with as many people as will listen,
and opportunities will bubble up for these same people to
help you move quicker and more effectively. Some of these
people will be full-time team members, some will share
nuggets of advice that impact your direction, and some
may turn into customers.

Your vision, combined with the feedback from
others, will begin to solidify a short list so that you
can **gather the assets closest to you**. For most, these
assets will be expert talent in software development and
marketing. But don't overconstrain yourself and the team.
Find capital, space, and existing assets that can help jump-
start your company. The key is to find those that are closest
to you and to make the ask. People want to help.

Keep balance between your vision and what you can
accomplish by **creating a short-term collective purpose**.
Try setting short-term goals and match your asset needs
with those goals. No plan survives the first contact with a
customer, so get something in front of someone as soon as
possible. Look for the minimum version of what you need
to create that initial customer feedback.

Creating a sustainable and meaningful company
is hard. That much is clear. But it is doable and I believe
that you can learn how to get started more effectively and
get through that first year. Maybe you will not achieve
Zuckerberg-like outcomes but you will be successful
nonetheless.

Lastly, build the fort.

Acknowledgements

I treated the writing of this book like a startup. Go figure ☺. To that end, there are many people I would like to thank.

Jimmy Doyle, Danny Moore, my brother Timmy, and Mr. Conti—thanks for being real life inspiration for the story. I remember the forts like it was yesterday.

Marshall Clark—we have built many a fort over the years. Thanks for being my foil and coining "our" term for startups: Build The Fort.

The Raleigh-Durham/Triangle/RTP startup scene is exploding and has served as my sandbox for the last five years. I have worked with some of the best founders including Tim Huntley, Jed Carlson, Mike Doernberg, Taylor Mingos, Tobi Walter, Jud Bowman, Ryan Allis, Joe Colopy and Chaz Felix, Justin Miller, James Avery, Robbie Allen, Ricci Wolman, Juan Sistachs, Jesse Lipson, Aaron Houghton, Henry Copeland, Brendan Morrisey, Eric Boggs, Matt Williamson, Brian Handly, and countless others. Closely aligned with the founders are Jason Caplain, Merrill Mason, Ted Zoller, David Jones, Glen Caplan, Justin Kasierski, Joan Siefert Rose, Brooks Malone, Bill Brown, Kip Frey, Jay Bigelow, Neil Bagchi, Dhruv Patel, Lee Buck, Tom McMurray, and Bruce Boehm.

My local club has some pretty special people, including Adam Klein and Casey Steinbacher. There is so much we have done together and so much more ahead. Larry Silverman, Jen Berger, Norm Santos, Megan Carriker, Courtney Gatter, Anthony Deloso, and Katie Page are all extremely talented friends who answered my call when I needed them.

Huge thanks to my partner in The Startup Factory, Dave Neal. It has been a great ride so far and I look forward to more. Our ability to consistently complement each other amazes me. Thanks for giving me the time to write this book.

Since a large portion of this book is about mentorship, I would be remiss if I did not call out some major mentor dudes who had a significant influence in my professional life. My uncle Doug Heivly started me on my computer-mapping path and my first professor, Wes Thomas, took it to the next step. We were partners, Wes. Dave Cowan taught me how to get stuff done. Thanks for being my practical not theoretical leader, Dave.

Richard Clarke is one of the most respected government officials I ever met and had the privilege of working with. Your dedication to our country and the sacrifices you have made while maintaining your strength was an awesome experience for me and my respect continues to this day.

Bart Faber taught me everything about business. Everything. Not a day goes by that I don't refer back to some small lesson and that internal voice that whispers, "What would Bart think?" I only wish you lived closer as you would enjoy this as much as I do.

As a first-time writer, you all know or can imagine the support you need from the publishing industry. Lisa Hagan and Beth Wareham, thanks for your confidence and support; I can't wait to work with you on the next book. You are my two newest, bestest friends a writer could have.

Lastly, there is family. Jess, Ashley, and Jake—thanks for being in my life. You all have turned into wonderful adults. I am very proud of each one of you. Mom and Dad, you set a standard for me; Tim and Marc, that obviously worked as you have very successful and grounded sons. Tim and Marc—thanks for being two of the best brothers a guy can have. I can't imagine a better family growing up. Patty, what can I say? Your unwavering support of every one of my crazy ideas and desire to work those ideas tirelessly has been awesome. You are the rock for me—without you I am nothing.

About the Author

Chris Heivly is one of the nation's leading experts in how to turn startups into multimillion-dollar companies. At a time when the nation's economy is shifting from a reliance on large corporations to smaller, more innovative organizations, he has been dubbed the "The Startup Whisperer."

For more than 30 years, Heivly has worked at the highest levels for some of the world's most recognized brands, including MapQuest, which was sold to AOL for $1.2 billion; Rand McNally, the world's largest map publisher; and Accenture, the largest multinational management consulting, technology services, and outsourcing company on the planet. He has also personally directed more than $75 million in investment capital on behalf of these and other companies.

Heivly currently serves as one of two managing directors of The Startup Factory, the largest seed investment firm in the Southeast. Under his leadership, the firm has made 35 investments in just three years in emerging technology companies. More than 60 percent of TSF's portfolio has gone on to raise follow-on capital, more than double the industry average for similar investment programs.

Heivly has become a sought-after speaker and go-to source for media. He has been quoted in major national and international outlets such as *Forbes, Inc.*, The *Washington Post, TechCrunch, Crain's Business Journal,*

Tech Cocktail, the *Financial Post*, and the *Montreal Gazette*, and has appeared in major-market TV stations across the U.S. Because of his stature in the startup world, he was heavily featured in the documentary *Startupland*, which showcased the world's most renowned entrepreneurs and startup experts. He is a contributing writer for *Inc.com*, the nation's leading entrepreneurial magazine for entrepreneurs and business owners, and has a significant following for Heivly.com, his own highly respected blog that offers brutally authentic commentary on startups and the startup community.

MY TED TALK THAT INSPIRED THE BOOK

http://tedxtalks.ted.com/video/Building-the-fort-a metaphor-fo

MY BLOGS

www.buildthefort.com
www.heivly.com
www.thestartupfactory.co
www.bigtop.it

BLOGS I CONSULT ON A REGULAR BASIS

www.feld.com
www.avc.com
www.bothsidesofthetable.com
www.andrewchen.co
www.firstround.com
www.bhorowitz.com

GREAT BLOGS FOR START-UP ENTREPRENUERS

www.steveblank.com

www.growthhackers.com

www.leanstack.com

www.zapier.com/blog

blog.kissmetrics.com

blog.bufferapp.com

www.quora.com

www.crunchbase.com

www.techcrunch.com

www.inc.com

www.angellist.com

news.ycombinator.com

Made in the USA
Monee, IL
23 October 2023